# Easy
# Weaning
## & First Feeding

Also available in the NANNY KNOWS BEST series

*Successful Potty Training*
*Stop Your Baby's Crying*
*Coping with Temper Tantrums*

# Easy
# Weaning
## & First Feeding

# Nanny Smith

### with Nina Grunfeld

LIMITED EDITIONS
BOOKTITLES

This edition published in 1996 by Limited Editions

First published in the United Kingdom in 1996
by Vermilion, an imprint of Ebury Press,
Random House, 20 Vauxhall Bridge Road,
London SW1V 2SA

Random House Australia (Pty) Limited
20 Alfred Street, Milsons Point, Sydney
New South Wales 2061, Australia

Random House New Zealand Limited
18 Poland Road, Glenfield
Auckland 10, New Zealand

Random House South Africa (Pty) Limited
PO Box 337, Bergvlei, South Africa

Random House UK Limited Reg. No. 954009

A CIP catalogue record for this book is available from the
British Library.

Printed and bound in Great Britain by
Mackays of Chatham PLC, Chatham, Kent

# CONTENTS

# AUTHOR'S NOTE

Unless a specific child is being written about, throughout the book your baby is referred to as 'he', not because of any bias but to differentiate you, the mother or child carer, from your baby.

# CHAPTER ONE

# Make Meals a Pleasure – Not a Problem

WHEN YOUR CHILD GROWS UP, IN THE BACK OF his mind there should be the happy mealtimes of his childhood to remember. Food is a child's first pleasure, to be enjoyed at first in his mother's arms, and later at the family table. Today, for a number of reasons, we have drifted away from traditional eating habits which is a pity because mealtimes should be enjoyed together. Of course sometimes you are in a hurry or the child may have tea and the parents have supper later, but it is rather nice if at least one mealtime can be eaten together a week, maybe Saturday or Sunday lunch. Eating together is more or less a social occasion and should be a time when everybody, including the child, is sitting down and enjoying the situation. It should be a time when people remain sitting down until everyone has finished and the child eats according to the stage he has reached. Breakfast, lunch, and tea should be civilised times and basic good manners should be adhered to so the child has something positive to copy.

## If he's hungry, he'll eat

Children enjoy food and if you are relaxed you too will get a great deal of pleasure from feeding your baby with a spoon and later watching him eat by himself. It is such fun when you first feed them with a spoon and they open their mouths wide time and time again. When they have had enough to eat they close their lips firmly and shake their little heads to say they don't want anymore. If a child is hungry he will eat his food and if he doesn't wish to do so, either because he has had enough or because he does not like it, respect his feelings and don't insist he eats it. Don't scold, don't bribe, don't withhold treats, respect the child's inclinations (see Chapter Two, Four Golden Rules). People do have battles with children regarding food which is unfortunate. The baby is unhappy and the parent is full of remorse and it is all unnecessary and unproductive.

I'm sure problems arise mainly with the first baby because mothers worry about what food to give the child, how much and when to give it and of course they will be given conflicting advice by friends, grandparents, clinics, whomever they ask. But babies are tough and I often think they put up with a lot from adults, but they all survive in the end — really you will find that some babies eat a lot, some don't eat very much and you can be guided by the baby himself. It is his own tummy, after all and if you offer him a balanced meal he will let you know how much of it he wants.

## Your child's problem — or yours?

All problems that children might have with food are really to do with your approach and the problems you might have about food, as I think the following case history clearly illustrates. (See also Chapter Six, Establishing Trouble-free Eating.)

*O*ne desperate mother contacted me because her two-and-a-half-year-old daughter was refusing all solid food and would only drink milk and juice out of a bottle. The child's doctor had told the mother that it was not a problem, her daughter was healthy and would eat when she was ready. But her mother was worried and embarrassed and yet was trying not to make a big issue out of it. Most food she offered her daughter, her daughter refused to try at all, but occasionally if she was tempted by something and started to eat it, she would immediately retch and vomit. Her mother was worried that she was anorexic or suffering from some other psychological problem associated with food.

This is one of the many cases when the mother has a bigger problem than the child because inevitably people she knows are going to discuss it, or have already, and she has been getting more and more fussed about it. I agreed with the doctor that children can go without food for a very long time, especially if they are having milk, as milk is the perfect food – it is very nourishing. The real problem here was one of social acceptability and I thought that probably when it started the mother had been over-anxious, and instead of ignoring it, her anxiety had transferred itself to the little girl. I told the mother that although the child was underweight, she was certainly not anorexic.

I suggested that at breakfast she should sit her daughter in her chair with her bottle whilst she and her husband eat their breakfast completely normally, without mentioning anything, or offering anything, to the child and do the same at lunch and at tea. As she had been told there was nothing physically wrong with her daughter I would have thought that within a few weeks of food not being offered to her the little girl might point and say 'I want some'. I told the mother that at this point she should not comment at all, but just cut a bit off whatever she is having and put it on her daughter's tray.

This is a situation when it is best not to say anything at all. I thought the daughter would soon do what her mother and father did. She wouldn't be having a bottle only by the time she was four or five.

But I did wonder why the daughter retched and vomited; I wondered if in her agitation the mother had put food in her daughter's mouth which she hadn't wanted.

Although at one time children were often forced to eat food when they really didn't wish to, now, with all this talk of slimming, children are very often, to my horror, refused food so they won't be fat. It must cause a lot of damage to a child's development to deprive him of food. People even worry about babies being fat and don't feed them in the night so they won't get fatter.

Of course you don't need to give them so-called fattening foods. Their sugar intake is something you can restrict. Children get enough natural sugar in fruit so I never give my children extra sugar. I do give them cakes, biscuits, jams and puddings which of course contain sugar, but I never add it to their cereal – and they aren't given sweets before they are two and then only a few Smarties. Of course, the younger children do get sweets and chocolates earlier from time to time because their older siblings have them.

**Food fads are for adults**

Children shouldn't be subjected to their elders' food fads; they should be allowed to have a properly fed childhood. If parents want skimmed milk that's fine, but children need whole milk for their physical development. People do the most extraordinary things to their children, presumably worrying about them being overweight and yet most of the children I have known who were really rather plump little people are now very slim adults. It is vital to feed children well and not keep them short of what they need. You are feeding them for the future. Children need plenty of nourishing, simple food for their development with no snacks in between meals. If you want a good plant you feed it and take care of it and that's like having a small child who's going to be an adult, you feed him and take care of him and with luck he will have good health when he grows up.

A child of two may begin to be more discerning about his food but even then he will have his own likes and dislikes – and they may well not be the same as yours, so let him have the opportunity to find out what he needs and doesn't need, likes and doesn't like. I hear parents say that they don't feed their child a whole host of things because he is 'allergic' to them – allergies do exist of course but are not nearly so common as people imagine. (See Chapter Seven, Some Possible Problems.) People say 'Oh, he's allergic to so and so' when actually what they mean is that he doesn't like it, or they don't think he does. Sadly most problems people have with babies have really been caused by an outside influence.

**Give him a job to do**

If you are like me and don't enjoy cooking it can be difficult thinking up a balanced diet for every day of the year and then preparing it. However with the advent of deep freezers things have become much easier. If you aren't a natural cook you may find it even more annoying to have the child around while you are cooking, but some children may enjoy helping with simple tasks like washing potatoes or stirring the cake mixture once it is almost finished – one task keeps the child going whilst you cook the whole meal. You may find you enjoy the cooking more too with a little person to keep you company. (Some suggestions for lunchtime menus for young children are given in What to Feed Your Baby, pages 86-93.)

# CHAPTER TWO

# Four Golden Rules

I HAVE ALWAYS ENJOYED FOOD ENORMOUSLY. IN THE family circle there was a joke about food being my hobby because I did enjoy it so much. I suppose that is why I have never had any problems when feeding children. I expected them to enjoy their meal – as I would do – and they either did or occasionally they didn't, which didn't matter. But if you sit eating peacefully together with your child, not talking about the food, or the mess, or the amount the child is eating or not eating, your child will enjoy his meal too.

*The First Golden Rule is:*

### ✦Let them enjoy their meal in peace
(don't talk about eating)

Adults love talking about food but, as with everything else concerning the child, never talk about what the child is or is not eating – or how much – to other people, especially not in front of him. It's best not to talk about food at all. As the child gets a little older, keep off the subjects of fattening foods, calories, slimming diets, food allergies etc. in his hearing. They're not suitable topics for discussion in front of children and could lead to their developing eating problems in the future.

People often say to children 'Now, what would you like to eat?' but it is so much better for everyone if the food is produced and they eat it or they don't. I always give children small helpings initially and I never criticise or praise the amount they eat. (See Chapter Six, Establishing Trouble-free Eating.)

## Feed him on his own
There was a strict rule many years ago that children were never allowed to speak at table unless they were spoken to. Thank goodness that has gone, but it did mean that the children got on with their food and were not sidetracked. Babies especially need peace and quiet and a relaxed atmosphere when they first start solids, not being fed with the family whose talking may distract them and food possibly be offered that they might not be ready for. It is much more enjoyable for him on a one-to-one basis, the mother feeding the baby before the main meal. He will then be relaxed and happy, his tummy will have been filled and he can either go to sleep or play quietly whilst you enjoy your meal. In no time at all – somewhere between the ages of one and two, he will be joining the family meal but it makes a good and easy introduction to mixed feeding if he can have you all to himself as he is introduced to the new food.

## Don't criticise his messy ways
When a baby starts mixed feeding it is what you could safely call very, very messy. However, you have to continue feeding him no matter how messy the situa-

tion might be. The mess does worry people and I have seen them wipe the baby's mouth after every spoonful. This, I think, is wrong – the baby should enjoy the food and not have his face wiped until the end of the meal. Being messy is not something he understands – children very often are so intrigued by a bowl of food they put their hands right in it. One of my little girls used to put her hands into the food and turn them over and over and cover them in the food – as if she was washing them in a bowl of water. I completely ignored this and when we got to the end of the dish I just scraped the food off her hands if I needed it to feed her with, otherwise I left it and at the end of the meal I would wipe her hands so the food didn't go everywhere.

**Allow enough time**
It is very important to stick to regular mealtimes and allow enough time for them, because then you know that when it gets to a certain time that that is the time to feed the baby; you know it takes half an hour because babies do eat such little amounts at a time so you can allow the half an hour. I always tried to aim for everything being unhurried. You may wish your child would get on and hurry up, but trying to keep everything on an even keel makes for a much happier childhood.

### The Second Golden Rule is:

### ✦ Don't hurry the meal
(or push the child before he's ready)

Just as the meal should not be hurried, so you must try not to get impatient and attempt to speed up your child's development. I have always worked on the idea that each stage should be taken slowly. With weaning, for instance, it is best for both the child and the mother to spread this out over a number of weeks (see Chapter Three, From Sucking to Sipping). Similarly, when it comes to mixed feeding, a child must be given time to acquire the necessary skills.

I have seen small children being given spoons and forks much too big for their mouths. It is so unkind – the implements are unwieldy and the child can't cope and invariably drops them or sticks the fork in his face. I have seen children scolded for not being able to cope with cutlery that is much too big for them. A child should use a teaspoon until he is three or four when he can be given a small fork. (See Chapter Four, Equipment for Mixed Feeding.)

## What's wrong with being a baby?

If children are ready then you can move on, but if not, then don't hurry them. I always put a child in a bib until he was four, but one of my children wore a bib until he was almost five because when he was eating he always spilt food down himself. If anyone remarked on his bib I always replied 'When he's taller he can have a napkin but it would fall off his knee if he had it now'. I get so angry when I hear children say 'I don't wear a bib, babies wear bibs'. Obviously someone has said this in their hearing. The point of wearing a bib is to protect your dress or shirt and children hate having napkins pushed into the top of the dress or shirt, it is so uncomfortable or it falls off and the food goes down their clothes. (See Chapter Four.)

I often continue a particular routine for what some people might call 'a long time', for example I always keep a child strapped into a high-chair until he is two and a half years old. It might seem rather late to some people but at this stage a child is very adventurous, energetic and agile and can climb; if you suddenly have to leave the room for some reason then if he is strapped in you can happily do so. If children have always been strapped in they will never query it, they will always lift their arms up to be strapped in and accept it. If they aren't strapped in the moment you leave the room they may wonder where you have gone and stand up to follow you and it can be extremely dangerous – they could knock all their teeth out or break an arm.

## Let him develop at his own pace

So many things are offered these days to 'push' children in their development. They are sold to anxious parents and they are quite unnecessary. A child develops at his own pace and in many cases it may even be harmful or regressive to try and make him go faster. I've known people to introduce food to small children when they are really not quite ready for it. I've seen babies given ice cream or a similar very cold food and they have shuddered from the shock of the cold temperature. It won't put them off eating anything else, but it may not be very good for their tummies.

People sometimes boast that their child eats 'the same as us' when he is still under two years and should not yet be eating the same food. Babies and toddlers are so happy having nursery food and although for first-time parents it is difficult to appreciate that very soon a child will be eating more or less the same as them, it is important that he should be allowed to go through a phase of eating the simple nursery food that he enjoys and is also so much easier for him to digest. Of course if a family is all eating together a child will become interested in what they are eating and point to it and if it is not too spicy there is no reason why he shouldn't be given a little bit to try. Quite often he will spit it out as he hasn't liked it, but he should be allowed to try it. But don't rush him, in such a short time your child will be doing all the same things that other children do and eating the same food as you.

**Force feeding**

Long ago if children didn't eat the breakfast that had been given to them it was produced at lunchtime and sadly if it still wasn't eaten then it was produced again at teatime. I suppose in the end the child was so hungry that out of desperation he would have eaten it, but this is an example of the parent or the nurse having a feeling of power. I never make a child finish what is on his plate or force him to try something he doesn't want to. Why should he?

## The Third Golden Rule is:

### ✦ Never force a child to eat
(mealtimes should not be battlegrounds)

I remember someone once saying to me that her children never wanted to eat Brussels sprouts but she always insisted they ate one. I was amazed. I thought it obviously gave her a feeling of power over the children. What drives me mad is children being forced to eat food they don't want. What's the point of forcing a child to have a tiny bit of carrot or one sprout? It's so aggressive and unnecessary. If they don't want to eat it then say 'That's all right' or don't comment on it at all and don't give it to them.

As children get towards two years they will start having likes and dislikes and you will notice them shuddering as they eat certain foods that they dislike. Sometimes, they will spit it out. Sooner or later they will tell you they don't like eating so-and-so, but if you notice them shuddering then I would not give it to them again as this might build up a resistance to eating. I wouldn't comment either – we all dislike certain foods, why can't they?

## *The Fourth Golden Rule is:*

# ✦ Although small, your child is an individual
(he has his own likes and dislikes)

It is quite possible at some point that the baby will not want to eat a particular food and this does actually worry people, and hurt their feelings – they have made this lovely food and the baby doesn't want it – but if the baby doesn't want it it is important not to give it.to him

## *Children know what they need*

Nature really dictates what the body needs and some foods that small children, and indeed adults do not eat, are foods the body is rejecting as unwanted, not needed. I was rather amazed when one of my little girls ate most of the eggshell as well as the egg (she also ate the blackboard chalk) but she did really need the extra calcium that she obtained from both the eggshell and the chalk. She had very poor quality teeth and her body knew what she needed and so when anything was available that would help, she ate it.

It is a fact that children, again like adults, enjoy some foods more than others and will eat the things they like, or need, first. I always provide a balanced meal for the child, with a little protein, a little starch and some fruit or vegetables and then they eat what they want and really what they enjoy is more or less what their body needs. (See Chapter Six, Establishing Trouble-free Eating.)

## Don't cajole him into eating

Eating time is a social time, but it isn't a game and you cannot blame little children if you started it as a game ('One for Mummy . . ') and they want to carry it on as a

game. People have always done that; if the child is a
slow eater and turns his spoon over so he loses the food
from it, it is very tempting to say 'Let's put the train in
the tunnel, open your mouth – here comes Thomas the
tank engine'. I have been slightly guilty of this myself,
but in retrospect I wouldn't start it. The child is enjoying the food but is taking his time about it so you
distract his attention and he opens his mouth and you
can put the food in. I wouldn't advise it or condemn it,
it is fun for the child and can speed things up but it can
become quite an annoying routine that you have to
stick to as the child is expecting it and looking forward
to it. It's amazing how many people do resort to these
devices and if your child doesn't want to eat then he
needn't eat and this shouldn't be used as a way of
making him eat. It's not fair. But if it is just that the child
is being slow and you want to try and speed him up
then it can be a useful way to distract him. I have seen
people make patterns – elaborate faces on sandwiches
etc. – with the child's food to tempt them to eat more
or, if they haven't eaten any, to eat some. This is
something that is so unnecessary, a time wasting
exercise on the parent's part. If the child is provided
with food that is well cooked they will eat it, if they
want it.

# CHAPTER THREE

# From Sucking to Sipping – The Easy Way

THE WORD WEANING HAS TWO MEANINGS: THE FIRST, causing a baby to accept other nourishment in place of his mother's milk, and the second, causing a change of habit, as when someone says 'I'm trying to wean him off his dummy/Tintin book' or whatever. When I was training, weaning meant specifically going from liquid to solid food, but it is also much used now in the other sense of when the mother wants to steer the child away from something. In fact both meanings share the idea of changing from one thing to another.

## *Weaning from breast to bottle*

Babies used to be weaned from the breast or bottle on to solid food at about nine months, so breast-fed babies had quite a long stint at the breast and all babies had a good long time to suck. I trained as a nursery nurse in a mother and baby home. It was a home where

unmarried women came to have their babies and all the
mothers breast-fed their babies and carried on doing so
when they took them home, unless there were very
special circumstances, but if a mother left her baby in
the home with us then he was weaned from the breast
to the bottle at a month old.

## Some don't want to breast-feed

There are various reasons why people stop breast-
feeding. Today the main one is of course, going back to
work, but the mother might also be put on a certain
medication which shouldn't pass through to the baby.
Some women in any case do not like breast-feeding as it
is so time consuming and quite painful to start with, so
they either don't do it at all or just do it for a short time.
I've known mothers who can't bear to sit there when
they could be doing something else. Babies get furious if
you do something else when you are feeding them – they
want your full attention. Feeding a baby with a bottle
takes just as long as feeding with a bosom but very often
the mother becomes more tired breast-feeding so to stop
is a release from what may be becoming a chore.

## A sense of loss

Of course, some women do like breast-feeding their
babies very much and hate stopping. It's such a cosy
situation and also the baby is relying on them and so it
gives them a feeling of being needed. I've known
mothers breast-feeding their two-year-olds, especially
when they knew it was going to be their last baby, as
though they wanted the intimacy to carry on forever, to
continue sharing something which excludes the rest of
the world. I think mothers ending breast-feeding may
feel quite sad because even though they may have
thought of it as a chore, once it is over they get quite
nostalgic and wistful about it.

There is another, more positive way of looking at this. The end of breast-feeding is a release from an hour of feeding and changing a nappy, so that is a plus; you can also now enjoy them for themselves rather than having them solely dependent on you. All the changes are enjoyable. With that hour free you can begin to be yourself again, you are not tied down and if you are busy someone else can feed your baby. It will also be very cosy with the bottle, different from the breast and less exclusively intimate, but very close and loving. They look up at you and are so grateful.

## Weaning the gentle way

I think it is better for a mother as well as for a baby if breast-feeding is stopped slowly rather than abruptly. It will help her get over her sadness and help the baby adjust to the bottle. Doing things gradually I think is the kindest way all round.

I would substitute one bottle-feed for a breast-feed every week which means it will take five weeks from start to finish. If you have to do it faster you can but one feed a week is a good way for you both to get used to it. In the first week I would suggest stopping the 10 a.m. feed. You have fed him early in the morning which has been a very good feed as he hadn't had anything all night and you don't then have to feed him again until 2 p.m. The next week I would drop the 6 p.m. feed. That way he is still alternating bottle- and breast-feed. The third week I would drop the 2 p.m. feed, then a week later the 10 p.m. feed and then in the fifth week I would finish the 6 a.m. feed.

The speed of the weaning will so much depend on both you and the baby. You can be guided by the baby, after one breast-feed has been dropped he may want to drop them all, or he may cling even tighter to the remaining ones; you would have to see.

## Will my baby like a bottle?

Some babies really take to a bottle like a duck to water and some hate it so much they scream and scream and do not want that teat in their mouths. A dear little child I used to go to would not take the bottle from her mother and not even from me, she minded terribly. Her mother thought that if she was hungry she would take the bottle, but she would not.

If your baby refuses to suck you can understand why he might be doing this as a bottle is so alien to him. If he is an older baby, three months or over, you can give him a little milk from a cup or spoon so that he won't go hungry, but if it is a smaller baby who refuses to take the milk from the bottle then you have to persevere. If he absolutely refuses the bottle then you have to give up trying that particular feed and wait until the next feed. Try giving him the next feed a little bit earlier than you usually would and sooner or later hunger will drive him to the bottle. It does seem cruel but if you simply must give up the breast then the baby has to get used to the bottle.

## What to do if he refuses

At first babies do get so confused by the teat because it isn't like the nipple, but if for the first few feeds he can be fed by the father or the grandmother or a friend where there is no smell or association of breast milk then I think it would be a very good idea. If he refuses to take the bottle with them too you can try different shaped teats (try one that looks as much like a nipple as possible). You can try making the hole in the teat just a little larger than usual – if it is too big they choke – by stabbing it with a red hot needle. Alternatively you could buy a teat with a bigger hole and at first express some of your milk into the bottle so the baby can at least get the same smell and taste until he is used to sucking from the bottle. So, when he is being fed you can tentatively squeeze a drop or two of the familiar milk into his mouth to tempt him into sucking. I always used to boil teats and bottles to sterilize them so you could try that if you think an older baby might find the smell of the sterilizing solution off-putting.

## How will I feel?

I would think dropping the first feed will be the most difficult for you; it is the end of a routine with the baby and the baby is part of you and quite often mothers are very sad although a few are greatly relieved. At first your breasts will feel extremely uncomfortable because Nature makes them fill up for the baby to feed, but as you feed less they are stimulated less and in a day or two it won't be quite so painful. You can massage a little milk out and that too will relieve the fullness.

## Part-time weaning

If you don't have to, you don't need to wean the baby entirely. I have known mothers who just wanted to keep on the night-time feed and this should be possible – it almost always is. Lots of mothers express milk from the breasts if they have to be away all day or if indeed they go to a job for most of the day. If you feel very strongly that although you must go to work you are sorry you are not breast-feeding you can try expressing breast milk so it can be given to the baby in a bottle by someone else during the day. It is the ideal way if it is possible, but babies are very, very adaptable and you can feed your baby during the morning and evening and he can be fed by formula during the day. People who want to give up a couple of feeds rather than all of them do achieve this, and if you have done this then weaning him entirely will be much less of a problem.

## Sucking is so comforting

I have met people who have proudly said of their four-month-old 'He doesn't need a bottle anymore, he has a spoon and a cup'. It seemed to me so wrong, babies get their food and their comfort from sucking. It is ideal if you can leave the child to suck the breast or the bottle until he is nine months but to slowly introduce the cup before then for some of the feeds. This way, by the time he is nine months he has the cup entirely, (see Chapter Five, Starting Solid Foods). The point is to do everything gradually and to remember that a child does need to suck when he is small – it's a form of comfort as well as a form of food.

### Why can't he go on sucking?

At nine months the child does start rebelling against various things. He is now able to eat food from a spoon and drink from a cup and if you do leave him sucking the breast or bottle, even for another month, he will be loath to give it up. At nine months he is developing his own personality and beginning to be able to do more and more things. He is obviously unable to express himself in words but will start to rebel against change. So if most changes that have to be made can be made leading up to nine months he will be perfectly happy with a change of routine which if it were introduced after nine months he would not accept so easily.

### Don't leave it any later

Children feel secure if things are always the same but up to nine months any gradual changes are accepted and the child is quite happy about them. If the bottle or the breast are slowly removed before nine months the child doesn't seem to mind. If you do it gradually they gradually get used to it and they forget. They don't refuse to have the mug, they are getting something to drink and that's all they mind about. Any changes after ten months are much more difficult. Some mothers don't really mind if they can't make changes. I've met people who breast-fed their children until they were running about – I remember a three-year-old lifting up her mother's jumper for a suck – but why not, unless there suddenly was another baby and the first had to be weaned at a comparatively late age, which would be a problem for him? I see children of three or four sucking bottles and if the parents don't mind then it's all right, but it is a nuisance and so much easier if the child starts fitting into the ways of the household. I also know people who have been very embarrassed about their child still having a bottle at that age and yet they don't know what to do about it. In despair they only allow it at bedtime and that is terrible, it's as though the bottle is almost a sin (see letter below). And the child does get terribly upset if you forbid it – the bottle or breast has become his comforter – you now cannot remove it from him until he is ready to give it up.

*A* mother had a great problem because her two-year-old son was still drinking milk from a bottle and he was being ridiculed and her parenting skills questioned. She gave him his first bottle of the evening at 6 p.m. when she returned from work and then she gave him a further two bottles before he slept at 8 p.m.. He then woke two or three times in the night and had more bottles. He wasn't allowed milk during the day.

This is a problem that can easily evolve if a child is left with a bottle after the age of nine months. If you leave children with a bottle they become very attached to it, it becomes their comforter and it is not the milk they need, but the comfort of the sucking. But having a bottle as a comforter brings many problems. The main problem is that, if the bottle is filled with anything other than water, it can cause tooth decay. Other problems are that it fills up the child's tummy leaving less room for food and that, as with a dummy, if the child loses it in the night he calls out for it which is a tremendous nuisance for the parent.

I told the mother that she shouldn't forbid her son milk during the day as it was so much a part of his life. She should buy him a special new mug and when she came home from work she should just put the milk in the new mug without talking about it and sit him on her lap and very cosily give him the new mug to drink from. He might be interested in the mug and happy to drink from it or he might get angry. If he does she would have to produce a bottle but I thought he would soon get interested in the mug. Even if he drinks from the mug he may ask for his bottle afterwards, in which case she should give it to him but persevere again with the mug, though not force it on him.

In the night if he woke up and wanted comfort she would have to carry on giving him a bottle. Once he had got used to the mug she might be able to offer it to him in the night too, but it would take time. Or she might find that if he were allowed bottles in the day he might not need to wake up for them during the night. As the bottle was his comforter it could not be taken away from him until he was ready to part with it which may be in a year or two's time.

## From breast or bottle to cup

Whether the baby is breast- or bottle-fed, at five months I begin to introduce milk in a cup at the 10 a.m. feed. He is presently having five bottle feeds a day, but by the time he is nine months old and drinking solely from a cup he will be having three meals a day (see Chapter Seven, My Tried and Trusted Routines).

When the breast-feeding mothers I knew changed from the breast to a cup they gave their babies formula in the cup rather than expressing their own milk for the cup feed. There is no need for you to do this, you can carry on giving the baby breast milk. It may be a good idea because your breasts will be full ready for the baby and if he is not going to suck you will be uncomfortable and also it is a taste he is used to and likes and it is good for him.

### Choosing the time to wean

You could use introducing milk in a cup as a time to start running down your milk supply, or you could express the milk until he is nine months old or a year and run it down then. Breast-feeding is very, very tiring so you might think this is an ideal opportunity to slowly give it up, but if you wish to carry on feeding him your milk, then why not? The easiest time to express milk is around the time of the feed, but you can experiment. By now you will know the way your body works. You may find it easiest to use a pump. When you do then finally wish to stop giving your baby breast milk, look back to the beginning of this chapter.

## Five months

By the time he is five months your baby will have been drinking a little diluted fruit juice every teatime from a cup for three and a half months so he will be quite used to drinking from a cup (see Chapter Five, Starting Solid Foods). People have said to me 'Won't he find the cup strange being used to sucking breast or bottle?' Of course he will find the cup slightly strange, but it has got warm milk in it which he will enjoy. Some babies do slightly query it because they know that after their bath they've always had a bottle or a bosom full of milk and it is a bit odd to have the cup now instead of at teatime and full of milk instead of being full of juice. Eventually they accept it and are happy to have it. You tip it in the way you have done the fruit juice and they will soon enjoy it. You hold the baby the same way, wrapped firmly in a nappy or towel, and he must still have the saucer under his chin or his clothes will soon be soaking wet.

**How to tell if he's had enough**
It seems a lot to expect that the baby will be able to drink his entire milk feed (approximately 150ml [5 fl oz] at this stage) from his cup but the previous feed was about 6 a.m. and so his tummy will be ready for another feed; if you take it slowly he will drink all or most of it. In no time at all he will be drinking everything from a cup. If you are bottle feeding then you will know how much milk your child takes and will just bit by bit tip the milk from the bottle into the cup.

If you are breast-feeding you will have to work out approximately how much milk to give him. We were taught to work on the basis that for every 450g (1 lb) of his body weight a baby needs 75ml (2½ fl oz) of food a day which was then divided into five feeds. So, you will have to work it out. Make a little drop more than you think he will want (remembering you are only giving him one feed in the cup – the other four from your bosom) and then when you have finished the feed you will know if the baby is satisfied or not.

**Why your baby might cry**
If he cries when it is all gone then he may need a little

more. He may be crying because he has taken great gulps and so has a little bit of wind in his tummy or he may be crying because he misses the bosom or bottle, but babies are tough and if he has had his tummy filled up with warm milk from a cup on the whole he will be quite happy about that. It may take a little time before you can put him down because if he is sucking from a bosom or teat the food comes more slowly than if he is drinking from a cup when he gulps it down and so he possibly may need to do a big burp. Keep him upright on your lap for a few minutes holding his tummy and his back very firmly but not tightly or he will bring the milk up again, or on your shoulder if he's sleepy, but either way keeping his body straight so the wind can go up or down. If there's a kink, it can't.

Before introducing another feed by cup I always give him a month before starting the next one. This way he is used to milk in a mug but he is having his good old friend back for all the other feeds.

## Six months

At six months I give the baby his 2 p.m. feed from a cup as well. He is still sitting on my lap, but is no longer wrapped up quite so tightly. Instead he has a large bib on to protect his clothes and free his arms. I hold the very base of the cup so the handle is free for him to hold and I encourage him to do so. You do have to hang on tight otherwise he will grab it and fling it. I still guide the cup into his mouth but it is helping him feel what drinking is all about. He will still be having three feeds from bosom or bottle. If you are breast-feeding you could now stop this feed or you could express your milk for it.

## Seven months

At seven months I start giving the 6 p.m. feed in a cup as well, so the baby is still having two bottle- or breast-feeds.

## *Eight months*

Very often by eight months the baby is sleeping longer so you can substitute both the 6 a.m. and 10 a.m. feeds for an 8 a.m. breakfast with a baby cereal made with milk and a drink of milk in a cup. So, if the baby is by now 6.75kg (15 lbs), he may be getting four feeds of 240 ml (8 fl oz) of milk a day (8 a.m., 1 p.m., 5.30 p.m. and 10 p.m.), although at breakfast and luncheon some of the milk will either be given on cereal or in puddings. Or, he may still be having five feeds of 180 ml (6 fl oz). He would get approximately the same if he was 5.4kg or 7.65kg (12 lbs or 17 lbs) – at this stage you go more by age than by weight. The 10 p.m. feed is now the last remaining bottle – or breast-feed.

## *Nine months*

By the time a baby is nine months, the importance of milk in his diet has diminished. If he is eating a good balanced diet (see Chapter 6) you need no longer worry about the amount of ounces of milk he is getting. I never give a baby a bottle- or breast-feed after nine months.

If your child does carry on waking at 10 p.m. and it is obvious he is hoping for a drink then I would give it to him in a cup. If he is very distressed and longing for the breast or a bottle then I think you would have to give in or you will both be up all night. But if he is eating a proper diet and having a calm day and calm bath and bedtime then he really shouldn't be waking at this time of night. When you go into him, keep the lights in his bedroom off, use the light from the landing to see what you are doing, and try and feed him peacefully. Don't start rocking him off to sleep, put him down when he is still awake, but drowsy. If he has had a warm drink he will be sleepy.

# CHAPTER FOUR

# Equipment for Mixed Feeding

S O MANY THINGS ARE OFFERED TO PEOPLE WHO ARE about to have their first child and indeed once their first child has arrived, I think as time goes by mothers come to realise that much of what they bought for the baby was unnecessary. Certainly children do not need a training mug or beaker or a special baby spoon. The things that are needed when children are starting out on mixed feeding are things to protect them, and you, from the food and later they will need a high-chair.

## Choosing a cup

When a baby starts drinking from something other than a bottle or breast he can drink from a perfectly normal small mug, preferably one with a thin rather than a thick lip. A mug made of plastic or silver, or something else durable is handy so that if it is dropped or hurled it won't break. Children don't need the strange tilted mugs or the training mugs with a lid and a spout that are on sale today – those are totally unnecessary and very difficult both to drink out of and to clean.

## Choosing a bowl and plate

It is fun to have a dish with a picture on it if the child is given it as a present, but a quite ordinary small bowl is all that is necessary. It is a great help, however, if the bowl has straight sides because it is easier for the child to scoop up the food. Best are the straight-sided plastic bowls with suction at the bottom that won't move about when the child is trying to scrape the food off and can't be knocked off the tray or thrown onto the floor. They are excellent because at the time when the baby starts eating solids he will have reached the stage of practising picking things up and releasing them – he cannot work out that if he hurls his bowl of food to the floor then the food has gone, to him a bowl is just one more thing to throw.

You do see bowls that are divided into three, but I think that is unnecessary. The bowls you can get are designed so the very hot water stays in the compartment below does keep the food warm but I am inclined to think that although adults enjoy warm food babies usually don't seem to care, to them food is food. I did have a bowl like that and the hot water compartment had a little stopper to keep the hot water in; I think it also had a suction bottom as well. It is useful, but not essential, and you must make sure that there is no way the water can come out and scald the baby if he is using it by himself.

You don't really need a plate for a small child because when it comes to the time that he has little sandwiches or biscuits you simply put them on the tray of the high-chair because a plate is very quickly hurled overboard.

## Choosing a spoon

For when you start feeding the baby I find a very small metal teaspoon, almost coffee spoon size, preferably with a long handle, is ideal. Babies have very small mouths and so the spoons they are going to eat from should have very small bowls. Once the baby has his own spoon he can have a small teaspoon too, with a short handle. I would always use a metal spoon rather than a plastic one. The special baby plastic spoons that I have seen on sale are often to my mind too big for the baby's mouth. Of course a hungry baby will take his food from anything.

## Choosing a knife and fork

I never give a child a fork until he is almost four or a knife until he is five – until then I cut up all his food. Children like to have knives and forks to be like everyone else, but they can't really grasp that you spear the food with the fork and then cut it with the knife. I have seen two-year-old children wrestle with adult sized knives and forks who have been reprimanded for not using them properly – I try not to look, it makes me so mad. Children tend to scoop the food up with their spoon and sometimes help it on with their fingers. Until he is heading for four a child should only be given a teaspoon. Then I would give him a small fork and when he is five I would give him a small knife. I certainly would not give a child adult sized cutlery until he was seven.

## Choosing cooking utensils

Where I was trained we steamed food for children but when pressure cookers became widely available I used them. They are very useful because everything can be cooked in the same pan and is cooked very quickly but some people find them rather alarming when the steam hisses out. Before the child starts eating the same food as the adults you can cook chicken, potatoes and peas all at the same time. They are marvellous really.

Until the child was eighteen months old we used to

prepare all his food using a Mouli, which made all the food squashy, or a metal sieve and a wooden spoon. A liquidiser or some sort of electric food processor is certainly more convenient as the sieve is always a little difficult to wash and you do have to make sure it is quite clean. Once the child was two I would just mash his food with a fork and later just cut it into small pieces.

## Sterilizing feeding things

When I started mixed feeding I always put the clean feeding spoon into the mug, and poured boiling water over the mug, filling it to the top and letting it pour over the sides. Then I waited for a few seconds, lifted the spoon out using a tea towel as the handle would be hot, poured the water out of the cup and then put the spoon back into the empty cup for a few minutes until they were both cool. You must make sure the mug and the spoon are quite cold or it can be very unpleasant for the baby. Plastic or china mugs, like the silver christening mugs that my children used, should be sterilized too. If you are pouring boiling water into a china mug put a metal spoon or fork in first and pour the water down it as the china may crack if the boiling water is poured directly on to it. I would sterilize both the spoon and the cup until the baby was nine or ten months old. After that he's sucking his fingers and meeting all sorts of germs anyway so you needn't be so careful.

### Keeping them sterile

Before seven months we were incredibly fussy. Once we had poured the boiling water out we would then cover the cup with a clean muslin nappy or handkerchief to keep the germs and flies and dust at bay. When the fruit juice or milk was poured in we would cover it again until it was going to be used. I kept this up until the baby was eighteen months old, but if your child is very agile and creeping and crawling about at nine or ten months old then you don't really need to be so stringent about scalding to sterilize and so on. However, you always have to remember that food breeds germs very quickly so that is why everything to do with eating should be very, very clean. If I was going on a journey I would sterilize the cup first and then wrap it in a muslin nappy or a clean tea towel or man's handkerchief for the journey. Ironing any clean fabric with a very hot iron just before using it to pack the mug in would help to keep it sterilized.

## Keeping the child clean

### The long towelling bib

When babies are breast- or bottle-fed I always put them in a long towelling bib which ties round the waist as well as the neck. I always tie the neck bow at the side – under the baby's ear – so that I don't catch any of his hair as I am tying the bow. A very long bib is a good idea because it catches any overflow and means you don't have to change the baby's whole outfit. When I start giving the baby a little fruit juice, or a first solid feed, on my knee I put him in the same bib and I have a muslin nappy folded cornerwise, or large, soft tea towel ready to put under the baby's chin and wrap right round his arms. I then put his right arm round my back at waist-height and my left arm round his shoulders to steady him on my knee. With my left hand I hold his left arm and with my right hand I feed him. If you don't do this he will grab the dish and the food will go all over the place.

### Plastic bibs with sleeves

When he goes into a high-chair, at about eight to ten

months, then I always use a soft plastic bib with sleeves. It should be long enough to go below the waist so that it covers his lap. It is useful to have a towelling bib on top of that, to soak up any spilt food or liquid that might otherwise slide down the plastic bib as he wriggles and make a mess. You used to be able to buy a towelling bib with sleeves that had a separate plastic bib inside which buttoned on to the towelling bib. We used to boil the towelling and just wipe the plastic. Nowadays you can buy them all in one which does mean they don't last as long because the plastic slowly hardens and then splits in the washing machine. They are also not as long.

### The bib that shelves the problem
Once a child is eighteen months old he doesn't really need to have a bib with sleeves, just a very large towelling bib because at that age he is feeding himself, or at least trying to, and so long as it covers his lap that is all that matters. If you can't buy bibs long enough they are easy to make, you just scoop a neck out of a towelling nappy and tie some ribbon on both sides. Or you can use those hard plastic bibs with shelves at the bottom which are useful for catching the food. Children don't seem to mind wearing them but I would feel they were not particularly comfortable to wear. You would make sure that the child is able to sit up straight before using them because they are inflexible.

### The bygone party bib
When going to parties with our children we always took a bib, we did in fact sometimes have special bibs in matching envelopes which we kept for parties. Nowadays bibs are not taken, nor are they provided so children spill food on beautiful dresses and shirts and either are reprimanded for being messy eaters or no one

cares which is a pity as the stains may be difficult or impossible to remove.

### Cleaning him after the meal

I always had a flannel handy on a saucer under the high-chair so that when the child had finished eating I could mop round his mouth and hands. I also folded a towelling nappy over one of the arms of the high-chair and then I could dry him afterwards and just lift him out. If you have the flannel and towel ready before you start and don't have to keep jumping up and down to fetch things, it makes for a much more peaceful mealtime. For the same reason I also prepared the pudding and kept it to hand so it was there when needed.

### Keeping everything else clean

When you begin mixed feeding and the child is on your knee it is a good idea for you to be wearing a towelling plastic apron with a bib. For reasons best known to themselves, when babies sit on your lap to be fed they turn their head sideways, not up – almost as if they wanted to be breast-fed and then the food around their mouths goes all over you. If the apron has a towelling finish it is softer for the child to sit on. He won't mind the plastic but towelling would be more comfortable.

Underneath the high-chair I always put a sheet of plastic, such as a cheap plastic tablecloth, large enough to allow for far-flung spills. It is easy to clean and I even used to put it on top of the lino we had in the nursery. It made for such an easy tidy-up, so the child could carry on playing without me having to wash the floor around him. I would just fold it over and over and pick it up and could wipe it over with a wet cloth later. Don't ever scold a child for spilling food. (See Chapter One.)

## *Where to sit your baby*

For the first three months of a baby's introduction to solid foods, the best place for him to sit is as close as possible to his mother. Sitting on your lap he is supported by your arm and sits more upright than if he were in a buggy or one of those sleep chairs, which must be better for his digestion as well as being so much more cosy. It's a continuation of being fed, now it is solids rather than breast or bottle, but the position of feeding is still the same and so there are not too many changes all at once. Feeding them in those chairs seems so distant and also so bad for the mother's back. If the baby is in your arms you don't have to bend and stretch and later, when he is in a high-chair he is level with you, his mother, so you don't strain your back.

**Choosing a high-chair**

In the old days high-chairs were always wooden and we would scrub them down once a week and make sure they were very, very clean. You could also turn them all into a low chair with a little attached table with wheels so you didn't have to pick it up to move it, you could just push it out of the way. It was low down and the baby could bang the tray with a wooden spoon. Making them in to low chairs was an added interest, it wasn't essential and yet we all used them, the children did enjoy them. If it was a day you weren't going out he could sit in that and watch you. In time the tray became plastic, with rounded corners, which made them easy to clean; now often the entire chair is plastic which is easier still. However, in the high-chair you see nowadays very often the back and the seat are padded plastic, which I don't really like because you get food in the ridges of the plastic and in the ridges of the buttons and so it is more difficult to clean. The plastic eventually splits so the chair doesn't last as long (our wooden high-chairs lasted for generations) so if you are planning more than one child this type is not a good investment. Little children are perfectly happy sitting in a wooden chair. A plain plastic chair is not only slippery for the baby to sit on but can also be sticky in hot weather. You could make a washable towelling cover to put on the seat and attach the four corners with strings.

I keep my children in a high-chair for a very long time, until they are about three or four, depending on their size, because I think it much easier for a child to eat from a higher vantage point rather than having his little chin resting on the table. I put him in the high-chair but remove the tray so he can sit quite close to the table. Once he is three or four I take him out of his high-chair and put him in a chair which looks like an ordinary adult chair except it has much longer legs.

**Eating away from home**
I have often used a plastic booster seat. You strap it on an ordinary chair and it has the same effect as putting three or four cushions on the chair so the child can be at a proper level to eat at the table. It is comfortable and very easy to take with you if you are eating away from home and the high-chair is too big to take. I have seen seats which clip onto the table but there are so few tables that one can use them on that they are really rather a waste of money.

All my children had a seat which folded flat and opened out into a little chair and tray which hooked over the back of an ordinary dining chair, so the child was the same height as the adults when we all ate at table. You could use them in trains, at birthday parties, at Granny's for tea – everywhere. They were heavy but they were so useful. We even used to use them in cars but not since the new seatbelt legislation.

# CHAPTER FIVE

# Starting Solid Foods – The Easy Way

S O FAR YOUR BABY HAS HAD BREAST OR BOTTLE MILK which is a familiar food and you must now start introducing food that will be strange to him. As with all changes it is so important to introduce these new foods and tastes slowly, offering a little at the beginning and gradually more. You can be guided by your baby – if he is obviously enjoying the new food and opening his mouth like a little bird, then he can slowly be introduced to a variety of foods. Before starting on solids at around six months he will need to have got used to being fed with a spoon and to drinking from a cup. If you introduce these to him very early, he will be more ready to accept it later on.

## *Four weeks: the first spoon*

When a child is one month old I introduce very diluted, warm rosehip syrup, which I give him on a coffee spoon or small teaspoon at teatime. Round about 4 p.m. is a good time as it is between the two o' clock and the six o' clock feeds. I use rosehip syrup concentrate (the kind intended for babies) and I dilute it even more than the manufacturers recommend. I suggest at first you give him no more than this, because you're not used to using a spoon for a baby and he's not used to drinking from a spoon, he's used to sucking. Don't fill it quite full or he will spill it. Most babies open their mouths very wide to let the spoon in and then try to suck it as sucking is how babies survive, and so you must put the spoon on top of his tongue – not a long way back, at the front of his tongue, just to hold it down, and very carefully slide a drop of the fruit juice into his mouth from the spoon. Some babies don't like the hard feeling of the spoon at all and it can take them quite a time to get used to this new way of feeding, others take to it as if they'd always had a spoon and it is really amazing that within a very short time all babies really do enjoy this.

Babies are very clever, and very soon they open their mouths wide waiting for the spoon, and then the next spoon, and so on. They will enjoy the warm, sweet taste of the rosehip syrup. Be very sparing with it at first as it is a new experience; fairly soon you will be able to give two or three spoonfuls. You mustn't be tempted to give too much, it is just a pleasant way of introducing him to a spoon. If you give him too much it will probably come up again. I have always started with diluted rosehip because it has a pleasant taste and he will drink it as he gets older and the sugar in it is natural, but you can introduce boiled water instead, as long as it is warm. To test the temperature and make sure it is not too hot, just drop a few drops on to the back of your hand as you would do with a bottle. Because I am right-handed, I hold the new baby so that he is almost lying down in my left arm. I put a long towelling bib on him and then, to prevent him grabbing the spoon wrap him in a folded muslin nappy (see Chapter Four, page 37).

This catches the drips and also holds his arms in position so that you can get the spoon in.

## Six weeks: the first cup

After a couple of weeks of drinking from the spoon, I introduce the baby to a very small cup or a little child's mug (see Chapter Four). It doesn't need to be very big as you will only be having a very little liquid in the cup. Again I give the child very diluted rosehip syrup round about teatime. As before I put a bib on the baby and then wrap him in a nappy or towel, under his chin and round his shoulders, and I put him on my lap and wrap my left arm round him. In my left hand I hold a saucer which I put under his chin to catch the drips. With my right hand I give him a drink from the mug. This has to be done very carefully. As you put the mug to his lips he will open his mouth because something is touching his lips and so then you tip the mug and tip in just a very little drop of the warm fruit juice. Some of it will dribble out which is the point of the saucer – you can then tip it back into the mug afterwards.

### Watch out for his tongue

When you first start a mug quite a lot does normally go into a saucer because after all he is used to a spoon tipping the liquid in. He won't drink like an older child and you have to watch his tongue because if it gets in the mug and the fruit juice goes under his tongue he won't be able to swallow it and so it will run out and he won't have got his lovely drink. So, when you start the mug you have to introduce it slightly onto his bottom lip and over the beginning of his tongue so you can tip in a little drop and he will swallow it. Very quickly the baby knows that this mug contains this very delicious drink and he will be quite excited and pleased to have it. You must certainly keep his hands out of the way or he'll grab the mug and will lose the juice. Before you use the saucer you will have poured boiling water over it, as well as over the mug, to sterilize them.

### Starting vitamins and flouride

Once bottle-fed babies are six weeks old I begin giving them vitamin drops. I always found that it is best to give them when the child is in the bath because then when anything is spilt it runs down the tummy and you can just wash it off. Until a child is much bigger, say three or four it is still a good idea to give vitamin drops in the bath – they do have such a nasty, oily smell. I started breast-fed babies on vitamins once they were weaned. Ask your dentist when to start giving fluoride, and how many drops.

## Six months

The modern way is that people are told they will know when it is time to introduce solids. This actually can be difficult and worrying for a first time mother. The mother is told that she will notice the child suddenly wanting more food, but if he is being bottle-fed I always automatically increased the amounts he was getting according to the weight of the baby (see Chapter Three, page 30) so he would be continually getting more food and be quite satisfied. Or, even if you didn't weigh him you could rely on him looking disappointed when the food had finished to tell you you needed to give him an extra ounce of milk a feed. You can follow the baby's lead and needn't weigh him, but if you do weigh him you will automatically know when he needs more food and so can pre-empt him ever being upset once a bottle has finished.

### Let him suck a little longer

If you are breast-feeding the sucking will stimulate

more milk and so you will probably be able to keep up with the baby's constantly increasing appetite, but if your baby does cry after a feed you can let him suck for five minutes longer. A baby who is replete will have a sleepy look about him and won't be searching any more. I think a hungry baby will probably be able to stimulate the supply of breast milk to match his needs and I would advise the breast-feeding mother to allow him to suck a little more until he was satisfied. Or, if she doesn't want to be sitting there for longer and longer, then I would advise her to wean the baby on to a bottle, because I do believe that babies should be allowed to suck until they are nine months old (see Chapter Three).

### Time to start solids

I always start mixed feeding at six months. By then babies are more observant, more alert, more alive and I always feel that it is time to introduce something other than sucking as a means of food. It is quite a good time to start. I have come across people who really didn't bother giving their child solid foods until they were a year old and then they had such trouble doing it, the child did not want to give up the bosom or bottle. Starting earlier I never thought was a good idea as it is very satisfying for a baby to suck all the food that he needs. I always thought that a baby under six months was not ready for solid food and doesn't really know what to do with it. By the time they have had half a year of sucking it is possibly quite interesting for them to start eating something on a spoon. By the time they are nine or ten months they are enjoying it.

One mother I heard from had a seven-and-a-half-month-old son whom she was still breast-feeding. At four months he had been given rice cereal but now would only reluctantly accept a

few teaspoons of the cereal three times a day
after a lot of head shaking and 'hassle'. The only
thing he wanted was food from his mother and
she didn't force him to eat but was wondering
whether she should because he was still waking
three times a night as he was so hungry. She was
quite desperate to get him off the bosom.

At four months it was too early really to
give him cereal, but I wondered why he had
taken against it so severely. I suggested that she
stop feeding him with a spoon altogether for two
weeks. That's a long time to a baby and she
would have to put up with disruptive nights and
possibly days as well as he might be very hungry.
She should try and feed him every four hours in a
quiet room – no television, no wireless, no visi-
tors and see if the sucking didn't produce enough
milk to keep him satisfied until she started solids
again. Then, two weeks later, without any fuss,
she should sit him in a high-chair, strap him in so
that he was upright and maybe put a cushion
behind him so that he didn't fling himself back,
bang his head and slide down, and I would then
introduce him to apple purée as if he was six
months old. It would be quite a new experience
for him to sit in a high-chair opposite his mother,
rather than having her look down at him, and he
would be quite interested. At the same time she
should start slowly replacing the breast with a
cup (see Chapter Three). I told her to take time
over this and obviously he would still like to suck
but he would be quite intrigued by having a
spoon and sitting in a chair and I should think
would have forgotten that he ever turned against
solids. It would be a whole new experience for
him to be apart from his mother instead of always

being in her arms being fed.

I also told her never to discuss the problem in front of him to him or anyone else. No matter how small a child is he can feel her anxiety.

## How to begin mixed feeding

When I start solids I am probably a bit over-cautious. I used to try just one spoonful of a new food. If the child lapped it up I would give him another spoonful but I would never force it on him. It is a new experience for the child and I didn't want anything to be a shock to his system. When you start giving your baby mixed feeding of course it is very, very strange for him to have a spoon put into his mouth with something solid rather than liquid on it. If you first hold the spoon next to his lips he will be interested by the taste and will open his mouth and lick the spoon a bit out of interest, then you can put it in. The solid food won't go straight down, it will stay in his mouth and he will turn it over and over and sort of suck at it. Occasionally the baby may push it out with his tongue so that it runs down his chin or else he will eventually make swallowing movements and it will slip down. I give him just one teaspoon because next to me his bottle is ready, being kept warm, so when he has had the first tentative spoonful then I pour a little of the milk into the cup and he has a drink from it (see Chapter Three, page 29). When the milk is finished I pour in some more until he has drunk it all.

## What do I feed my baby?

I always start at the 2 p.m. or lunchtime feed, by giving him one teaspoonful of cooked, sieved apple purée made from eating apples (if you have to use cooking apples you will have to add a little sugar) before his cup of milk and I have never yet met a baby who did not like it. I would give him that first teaspoonful, making it up to three teaspoonfuls once a day, at 2 p.m., for a week. Then, I would start introducing cooked, sieved carrot or spinach purée to bring in the changes, (see Appendix: What to Feed Your Baby).

I monitor all new foods carefully to make sure the baby does not have a reaction of any kind to them. It would be extremely unlikely that a baby would be allergic to simple food like that so there is no need to worry (see Chapter Seven). If the baby screws his face up and appears not to like the new food then I don't force it. Some babies don't like spinach as it is quite a strong taste. At first I always introduce a new food, by giving it two days in a row and then alternating it with other already tried foods.

Until he is nine months I always feed the baby on my lap, holding him in the crook of my arm, as he would have been if he was having the breast or a bottle. If you have another child to cope with then you can put the baby in the high-chair earlier with a cushion behind him and the straps on.

## What if he still seems hungry?

If you have given him one teaspoonful and he is very enthusiastic about it and has enjoyed it then you can give him a second one, but I wouldn't give him any more. When change is involved, it is much better to go slowly. I would produce the drink of milk and wait until the following day. If you attempt to give him more and more solid food then he won't have room for the milk and may not last as long between feeds. This would throw out your entire routine which may be important if you have a great deal to do and other children to look after (see My Tried and Tested Routines, pages 74-79).

*I* was once asked what to do by a mother who that week had started feeding her son on solid food and since then he had hardly stopped crying, all day and all night. He had never cried before. She thought the solids might have disagreed with him although he had so far only had apple – a teaspoon once a day as she had read in a book.

I told her that her son was probably hungry and she should increase the amount of apple and maybe start him on a little baby cereal as well. The crying stopped.

Once the baby has eaten solids at his 2 p.m. feed for two weeks I would introduce a little baby cereal at the 10 a.m. breakfast meal when he is already on a cup. I would make the baby cereal using some of the milk from his bottle of formula. If you are breast feeding then you can begin to use whole cow's milk (silver top) with cereals and in cooking, but the baby should not yet drink it. After a week of cereal at 10 a.m., I give him a little baby cereal in the evening at the 6 p.m. feed, again mixed with his formula milk or cow's milk, and followed by a bottle- or breast-feed. There is no need to buy lots of different packets of cereals. A fine, healthy baby enjoys the same cereal at the same time every day – just as some adults enjoy porridge every morning for years. (See Chapter Six, Establishing Trouble-free Eating.)

A mother once asked me what to do about her six-month-old baby who seemed to be very windy since she had started solid food and her mother wondered what she could do about this as she was worried the wind might be disturbing her daughter.

I wondered if she had been on rather an adventurous diet for such a little baby. I told her mother to stick to non-flatulent vegetables (carrots, spinach, beetroot, parsnips, potatoes, sweet potatoes etc) and not to give her too much of anything, even if she was enjoying it. At this age her diet should still be mainly milk. After she had eaten I suggested that if she seemed sleepy she should be put in an upright position on her mother's shoulder, or if not sleepy, sat upright on her mother's knee. She should be held very firmly upright (not squeezed) for at least five minutes and the wind should go either up or down. If the wind continues to be excessive I suggested a little drink of warm water after the meal would help. If the wind continued and her daughter's stools started smelling offensive I suggested the mother sought medical advice.

## How much should I give him?

You have to use your discretion about how much food to give your baby. When you are feeding him, let him dictate the pace at which he is fed. You don't need to wait for him to chew the food down, he will endeavour to suck and some of it will come out of his mouth, and some of it he will swallow. He will open his mouth again when he is ready for more.

When you start mixed feeding babies usually eat all that you offer and very often they peer in amazement when the dish is empty and look a bit surprised. This doesn't necessarily mean that they would like some more, they are just interested that it is all gone. If you did think they would have liked a bit more then you can give them some more next time.

## Too little rather than too much

At this early stage, however, I would err on the side of giving a baby too little rather than trying to force him to eat too much. You very quickly get an idea of how much your child wants. He is still having a drink of milk as well as the food you are now giving him so he will not need much food. Begin tentatively and then you can be guided by how much he is enjoying the food and can give him a little more. Don't be tempted to give him more than he wants because he must take his milk afterwards. Babies would eat and eat if you let them, if it's something they really enjoy, but then they need their milk and if their tummy is too full it will all come up.

## Seven months

When the baby wakes up at 6 a.m. I would continue to give him his bottle of milk, or his usual breast-feed, and then put him back to bed. This is very convenient if you have other children to get off to school because hopefully he will still be asleep as they are getting dressed and ready. I then give him his breakfast at 10 a.m. (baby cereals and a cup of milk) or whenever he wakes and has been washed and dressed. Lunch could then be between 1 p.m. and 2 p.m., offering a savoury first course and then a little pudding followed by a cup of milk. At 5.30 p.m. or 6 p.m. I would then give him more baby cereals and a drink of milk from a cup; this is when I start giving the 6 p.m. feed in a cup (see Chapter Three). And at 10 p.m. the baby would have his bottle or breast- feed.

## What should I give him now?

At this stage you really needn't worry about what your baby will be eating tomorrow because, if you gave a baby of this age the same food every single lunchtime it wouldn't matter to him. His chief source of nourishment is still milk (whether bottle, bosom or cup), but it is good to start on very small helpings of other foods because it is interesting for him and good for him to introduce him to different tastes (see Appendix: What to Feed Your Baby).

Once the baby has been having solids for a month

you can start giving him a more adventurous midday meal, although always a very small helping of everything. Little tins and jars were frowned upon when I first started out but they are now very, very good and can be useful because the baby only wants a very little to eat. I wouldn't worry that your child isn't getting good food if he eats bought food because often when food is cooked at home for babies half the goodness is lost. But, if you have prepared something for the family you can give it to the baby providing it isn't seasoned – take a little out before you add any salt, sugar or other seasonings and Mouli, sieve or liquidize it for him. Small portions can also be frozen. If, for example, you are having roast chicken you can just remove some of the thigh (without the skin) from the cooked chicken and then purée it with some plain boiled potatoes, or rice or pasta, and a boiled vegetable. Then, when the food is cold you can divide it into little pots or put it in an ice cube tray, label it clearly and freeze it for future use.

## How do I introduce new foods?

Start new foods slowly whether they are home-made or bought so you can see if your child has any adverse reaction to them (see Chapter Eight). Very occasionally when you introduce a new food the baby will notice the taste is different and may look rather worried because it wasn't what he expected. It doesn't mean he doesn't like the food, so just carry on feeding him when he is ready for the next mouthful.

His food should still all be the same consistency and taken from a spoon. Even if he does have a few teeth he should not yet be having 'finger food', which I only introduce at nine months. I do however hear occasionally from mothers who have already started (or *not* in this case) giving their children finger foods at this age.

One mother I met was very worried because her sister had casually given her seven-and-a-half-month-old daughter a chip and some potato crisps to eat. She had been petrified that her daughter was going to choke and didn't want to give her any food to hold at all. The daughter already had two of her lower incisors (bottom teeth). I told her she was quite right – at that age a baby is not yet ready for sharp or very solid food. In any case a child of that age needs something of better food value than potato crisps.

However I did reassure her that babies are pretty tough – sometimes you think they are choking when they are just coughing. If something has gone down the wrong way then the first thing I do is to hold both the child's arms straight up in the air and if that hasn't worked I also pat him between his shoulder blades with the flat of my hand. If the baby is choking, I hold him upside down by his ankles in my left hand and with my right hand I make a fist and firmly thump him between his shoulder blades. Remember, he is still very small. If he appears distressed take him immediately to the nearest doctor or hospital.

With an older child, I place him face downwards across my knees, with his head hanging down and slap him again and again between the shoulder blades. If the obstruction has not become dislodged you must take the child to the nearest doctor or hospital as quickly as you can, carrying him over your shoulder with his head and shoulders hanging down.

**Something to chew over**

At around seven months I buy my children a packet of very hard biscuits – you can still buy them. They aren't biscuits to eat as they never disintegrate but they are nice for the children to bite on as their teeth are coming through and make a change from a plastic ring. Each biscuit has a hole in the end of it and a little ribbon threaded through and the idea is that with a small safety pin you can secure the ribbon to the child's outfit so when he opens his little fist and drops it, it doesn't drop very far. The other type of rusks which you can buy tend to dissolve and break and are a worry because the child can get a piece in his mouth and choke on that. They should only be given to children who are sitting up. When I was training we used to make our own hard rusks by cutting thick strips of white or brown bread and putting them in the oven on the very lowest heat to dry out. They became ever so hard and didn't break or dissolve as the child gnawed them. If they did occasionally break off it would be a biggish piece and so the child didn't swallow it. We would give them to a child once he could sit up and would keep an eye on him.

## Eight months

If your baby is a very good at sitting-up, or for some reason it is getting too complicated to feed him on your lap, you can now sit him in a high-chair, otherwise I first use it when the baby is nine months. At the same time as I introduce the high-chair I start using a harness, the same kind of straps as I use in a pram. I fasten them at the back – that's vital because clever babies can undo them.

## Nine months

By now he should be eating a good, balanced diet and you need no longer worry about the number of ounces of milk he is getting, although I still give him two mugs of milk (about 120 to 150 ml [4 to 5 fl oz] each), one at the end of breakfast and one at the end of tea, and I make lots of milk puddings. After lunch he has a drink of cooled, boiled or bottled water. He will be used to having his drink after his meal. I never give children a drink before they have eaten or it fills their tummies up (see Chapter Six, page 73). He will usually drink all the milk offered during the day but it doesn't matter if he doesn't drink it. Once a child is no longer breast-fed I start giving him multi-vitamin drops every day until he is one year old.

## What milk will he be having?
Until he is one year old your baby will go on drinking formula milk only although you can cook with cow's milk and use it for his cereal. Some children drink more than one mug of milk but others don't like milk at all or only drink a very little. This you have to respect because really Nature tells them what they need. You can try giving them milk puddings but if they don't like them, then don't worry. Milk is not essential for survival and it is more worrying if your child is drinking too much milk to the exclusion of his food (see Chapter Three). There are of course some people who simply cannot accept milk, they don't like it at all or are even allergic to it. You will know if your child has this allergy and needs to drink soya milk.

## What meals will he now have?
By now the baby is no longer having breast- or bottle-feeds and should be waking later. When he wakes in the morning I give him a drink of fruit juice in a cup. Breakfast is between 8.00 and 8.30 a.m., lunch is between 12.00 and 1.00 p.m. and consists as before of a savoury and a sweet course with cool boiled or bottled water to drink at the end of the meal. Tea is between 4

p.m. and 5 p.m. when I would give him little postage stamp sized sandwiches without the crusts and a little fresh or stewed fruit or baby cereal, depending on the child's appetite. I don't then give him anything more until the next morning and would expect a baby by now to be sleeping through the night and no longer having his 10 p.m. feed.

**What finger foods will he now eat?**
As well as the bread strips which I bake (see page 55) I now give babies tiny little open-top sandwiches for them to pick up and pop in their mouths. I give them to children one at a time or they sometimes put too many in their mouths to be able to cope with them. Very soon one can put out half a dozen bits at once and they will eat them one at a time – being thin bread they don't take much chewing. But even so I would never leave a child alone with any 'finger food' in case a bit got stuck in his throat. I would also be very wary of giving a little baby raw carrots or cucumber or apples to eat. When they are a little older they can enjoy these foods but at this stage it is safer to stick to dried bread, or rusks which will dissolve in the child's mouth.

*A* mother of an eleven-month-old boy told me that her son would not eat anything with lumps in or 'finger foods'. He would pick them up but wouldn't put them into his mouth. She said he ate puréed food at most meals but every other day he would refuse a meal altogether. He liked all his food warm, even yoghurt. He already had six teeth and since she introduced solids would occasionally cry suddenly when she was feeding him for no apparent reason.

I told her that apart from tiny sandwiches I always give children mashed, sieved or puréed food until they are one year old, so I would leave

him a month to have the kind of food he likes to
be given, and then try again, very tentatively, to
introduce 'finger foods'. I don't think the eruption
of teeth has anything to do with it, puréed food
fed by a spoon is so much easier to eat. But I did
wonder if he might have had some finger food
that was particularly hard or a little sharp that
had made him fearful of it. I told her not to worry
and not to make a big issue out of it if he refused
a meal altogether, but just to take the food away.
She shouldn't substitute anything else and she
shouldn't talk about it, just remove it. Children
can go a long time without food.

I said that I always give small children
warm food and that it is only when children are a
little older that they enjoy very cold food such as
ice cream. However, although I would give him
warm puddings – semolina, rice pudding, tapioca,
baked custard and so on, I wouldn't warm things
such as yoghurt that are meant to be eaten cold.
If he doesn't like them at room temperature I
wouldn't give them to him.

I suggested that he might be crying for any
number of reasons – it could be because he has
another tooth coming through and which has just
been inadvertently hit with the spoon, or because
he doesn't want any more food and doesn't know
how to tell her. Or, possibly the food is sometimes a little too hot in places and that is why he
cries, or he has bitten his tongue and that makes
him shout. I have had children weeping bitterly
when the spoon seems to have hit a tooth – I
think it probably is that they haven't been used to
eating with a spoon for very long and they bang it
against their teeth and it hurts.
But I also wondered if her little boy needed more

sleep or more rest in a cot or pram. Children do go through a period of growth every now and again which manifests itself by the child crying easily and being tired.

## Beginning to feed himself

At nine months you can give him his own spoon to hold whilst you feed him at the same time with your spoon. Sometimes the baby bangs the spoon and the food flies everywhere. Of course he will try to feed himself with his spoon and will pick up the food and get it as far as his mouth – and then, for some reason, he will turn the spoon over and all the food will drop off the spoon and onto his lap, so he does need a large bib with sleeves. A nine-month-old baby needs a teaspoon sized spoon with as short a handle as possible, preferably one no longer than the length of his hand, so he is not forever poking himself in the eye. Allow him to make as much mess as he wants and whatever he does don't fuss about it or scold as it is very easy to clean up especially if you stand the high-chair on a large piece of plastic. Don't worry if he seems to spill most of the food, you're still feeding him with the spoon and he will open his mouth when he sees it coming. (See also Chapter Four, Equipment for Mixed Feeding.)

*A* father once asked me whether he should let his nine-month-old daughter feed herself. He said that his daughter tended to drop her spoon and fork and dive in with both hands.

I said that the child should be allowed to have a spoon, but that a fork could be quite a liability at that age. I suggested they each had a spoon and the father should continue feeding her at the same time as she was feeding herself. If she drops her spoon then the father should rinse it off and give it back to her. I said it didn't matter at all if she dipped her hands in the food. It is rather messy but it is a very short period that she will do this and you can scrape the food off her hands with your spoon if it worries you and put the child in a very large bib which covers all their clothing. All children in the end feed themselves although some are more adept than others. They are learning to do so and you should try not to fuss about it at all.

## One year

By one year a child will normally try and hold his cup by himself and invariably he will wobble it and spill a little. There is no need for a child to have a cup with a spout, he will soon be able to drink perfectly from a small mug or cup. To help your child learn to drink you could buy him a two-handled mug. These are so useful and are what babies always used to be given.

On a journey I would take the drink in a bottle with a screw-top lid and just pour a little into the mug when we stopped for a picnic. It is not good for children to be drinking all the time from spouts and bottles. Apart from filling up their tummies with liquid it is not good for their teeth.

### Moving to cow's milk

Once children are a year old they can drink whole cow's milk (silver top) straight from the milk bottle and there is no more need for formula milk. I have been told that a growing one-year-old needs at least 1,000 calories a day and he needs the goodness from the milk for bones and teeth being developed. He should not have skimmed or semi-skimmed milk. Even if a weaning baby is a little overweight I would still give him a little cereal if he liked it and one or two rusks a day to chew as well as fruit, meat and vegetables. If the parents are not fat I am sure the child will soon begin to thin down (see Chapter Two, Four Golden Rules).

Once the baby is one year old I give him multi-vitamins in the winter only until he is five. I give them to him from September to April or May because during the summer, with luck, we have plenty of sunshine and he won't need them.

## Eighteen months

Once a child is eighteen months I start cutting some of his food up into small pieces but still mince or mash the rest. I then mix the more difficult things to scoop up together with the easier things, like minced chicken in with the mashed potato, so that it is easier to eat with a spoon. Alternatively I would chop the food up very small so he could pick it up with his fingers.

You will know how good an eater your child is and how much help he needs, but always give more, rather than less help. By now he will usually be able to drink from a proper cup and attempt to feed himself with a teaspoon, although he may sometimes use his fingers instead. He will scoop up mashed potato with a spoon and pick up a piece of carrot with his fingers – he will cope very well. He may still drop his plate on the floor when he has finished his meal but will be eating quite happily.

### Give your child confidence

At this stage you want to give your child confidence about his eating skills and so the food should be as easy as possible to transfer from the dish to the mouth. You should not make a comment of any kind. Even saying 'Shall I cut it up for you?' is annoying. Better to cut it up beforehand, don't leave any decisions to him.

I still keep an eye on children of this age just to see

they are eating enough and if the food does spill I help them feed themselves until they get better at it. It is most important not to talk about what or how they are eating. I am strongly against making any remarks to another person present such as 'Oh, dear – he is messy' or 'Jamie doesn't like sausages'. One sees adults that don't have particularly good table manners but you don't remark on it and so the child should be free to enjoy his food and to cope with it as well as he can. When he has had what he wants just take the dish away, don't say 'Well, what about trying this?' because if he had wanted it he would have eaten it. I have had children that didn't eat certain things and as adults they eat everything – tastes do develop (see Chapter Six, page 64).

## Two years

Once a child is two I begin to give him little helpings of food so he can see all the foods separately and knows what he is eating. He will be beginning to like some foods more than others and so if he sees, for example, a pile of peas which he likes he may eat them all straight away. It is so much more interesting for him and he is managing the spoon so much better, although I still cut it up in small pieces so he can scoop it up.

## Three years and over

By now your child will be eating very much the same meals as the rest of the family only his food is still chopped up and eaten with a spoon. Once a child gets to four I give him a fork. (See Chapter Four.)

At this stage I don't mention manners because on the whole a child should learn manners from the adults he is with. If you behave politely and considerately your child will copy exactly what you do – so it is essential that you do set a good example.

# CHAPTER SIX

# Establishing Trouble-free Eating

FEW THINGS CAUSE MORE ANGUISH IN THE HOME THAN people's eating or, worse still, *not* eating habits. This of course applies to children and adults. There's a lot of chat about what he or she does or does not like and a lot of discussion about how to 'make children eat'. Lots of threats and so on which do cause a lot of unhappiness for a child. In fact the less fuss that is made at meal times the sooner any so-called 'eating problem' is resolved.

### If he won't eat, ignore it
Under the age of two a child will eat practically everything unless he has elder siblings who he copies. If a small child doesn't want to eat his main course then just take it away but don't provide a substitute, not even a slice of bread and butter, and don't mention it. Quite often a child will not eat the first course but will always enjoy the pudding and sometimes having had the pudding he might then eat his first course. I have met

people who said 'If you don't eat your first course, you can't have your pudding'. This is monstrous. The important thing is not to make any fuss at all. If a child says 'I don't want this' then casually say 'Then don't eat it'. Don't get angry. Food should be enjoyed by children, not represent a threat.

**Tastes change**
If you are relaxed about a child not eating something, very often after a few weeks he will accept it, but even if he doesn't, there's no need to run around trying to buy him the one brand of special food he likes. It's quite unnecessary to try to disguise foods or buy special foods for your child – just provide good food and if he doesn't want to eat it he needn't. Of course, if he really doesn't like fish then I wouldn't cook it for him until he is a little older. Tastes develop and in the end he may like fish. When there is an older brother or sister the situation could become more difficult if you allow it to. It's as if the older child is testing out how much you will do for him by saying 'I don't want that. Can I have baked beans?' If that happens, just say 'This is what we are having today. We'll have baked beans another day'. Otherwise, if you pander to a child you cause an awful lot of extra work for yourself.

*I* get many worried letters from parents who have pandered to their child and are now regretting it. One typical query was from parents of a three-year-old who had never had a very large appetite and would now only eat a very limited variety of foods, such as fish fingers, chips and breakfast cereals.

I reassured the mother, that although it was a nuisance for her the child's health would be fine. I told her to avoid battles with her son and not to ask him what he would like to eat, just give herself and the rest of her family the food she has prepared for them and give him what she knows he likes and don't discuss it. One day he would say 'Why have you got different food from me? Why can't I have the same food as you?' and the problem would be resolved.

## Be guided by your child

Nature tells children what and how much they need to eat to run their bodies efficiently. It tells us when we are older as well, but we ignore it and eat more than we need of some food we really enjoy and very often regret it. A child will just take what he needs - he hasn't reached the stage that because he has enjoyed it he will have just one more spoonful. He has had all he needs and so he will just stop. Even if you don't think he has had enough you must respect him – he know best.

When you have got to the stage of two courses, main course and pudding and they don't want to eat all that you have prepared for the first course you can then offer the pudding – you can be guided by them. They may not consciously want it, but it may contain things that their body needs which were not in the main course and so they will eat it. One of my children often went for several days without eating his first course, only his pudding. It must have been the vitamins from the fruit or the calcium from the milk in the puddings that he needed – one doesn't know, but the child's body does. So it is very important to present children with a good, nourishing meal and let them choose what they need from it (see Appendix: What to Feed Your Baby).

Quite often children don't like certain foods such as cabbage. I myself could live on cabbage, but it is what you would call a rather windy vegetable, so when children refuse a particular food such as this they are not doing it to irritate you, they are doing it because Nature is telling them they don't need it. For instance, most of us enjoy leeks, but they are something children do not like – leeks also tend to be windy. Even though they can cause wind, peas are enjoyed by children on the whole because they are very attractive looking and easy to eat. Carrots are usually enjoyed either raw or cooked because they are sweet. My mother always used to steam vegetables so they were never over-cooked – they were delicious.

## Don't give him a choice

Small children are often asked what they would like to do, what they would like to wear, what they would like to eat, but it is much kinder if you make the decisions yourself. Simply provide a delicious lunch and sit the child down to it. If he eats it, fine, if he doesn't, fine. If you do ask the child what he wants to eat he may say 'I'd like a sausage' then, when you have provided what he asked for, he says 'I don't want this' and then you say, 'But you asked for it'. But that was twenty minutes ago, or even half an hour and it was just chat. That minute he might have wanted it and if the sausage had arrived at that moment he would probably have eaten it, but half an hour later he has changed his mind. Children live very much in the present. A very small child might just say 'sausages' or 'egg in an egg cup' as a sort of a game, it might well be the only name of a food he can remember and he just says something that is eatable rather than understanding that he's being asked to make a decision.

## Plan the menus yourself

It is so important to make the mealtime decisions for your child – it makes for a peaceful, happy, relaxed atmosphere for all concerned. If you can introduce the idea early on that the food is always there and he never chooses it then there won't be any battles. It has always been like that and he won't say 'But I wanted hamburgers' when you have presented a baked potato because he has never been consulted. If you have always asked him what he wants and then one day you then decide to make a meal without consulting him as to the menu, he may well say 'I don't want that, I want such and such'. So, it is best never to start asking him. Being given a choice is so confusing for small children who must feel secure – must know that everything goes on the same. Of course I don't mean that every single day he should have semolina pudding for the second course, I mean that every day he should have something delicious, something he would enjoy that you have chosen. You are in charge – as far as the child is concerned he can rely upon you to make sure all is well in all things.

*I* once visited a little girl of almost three who was given four or five bottles of milk a day to drink and very little else. Each meal time her mother stood by the fridge and said to her 'What do you want to eat? Chips? Pizza? Pasta?' but never actually produced any of the food. The little girl would say 'I want milk' and so her mother would give her a bottle.

  I told the mother that milk was reckoned to be the perfect food and so there was probably no need to worry about her daughter's health but that she was certainly old enough to start having a smooth and easy transference to solid foods soon. At mealtimes food should be prepared and put on the table. I said I would start at breakfast by serving her a bowl of milky porridge and a cup of milk. If she didn't want to eat it and insisted on the bottle then her mother should bring a bottle with only, say, 120 ml (4 fl oz) in it so that the child was hungry by the next meal. She shouldn't be given anything until lunch, then offered a little mashed potato, some mince and a vegetable followed by a milky pudding and a mug of water at the end. If she didn't want to eat and asked for her bottle then her mother should give it to her – again just half full. Then, at tea she should give her some tiny sandwiches and milk in a mug. This time I would give her her entire bottle if she asked for it at bedtime, if that was when she had it. I told the mother not to comment or criticise if her daughter didn't want to try any of the food but to ignore it and to continue making the meals. If she carried on like this after a few days her daughter would probably start eating a little.

## Let Daddy do the spoiling

It does seem to me to be the easy way out to ask a child what he would like to eat. It somehow shifts the responsibility of child care on to the child and I think people who do this are a bit lazy. Once children had turned five, one of my families always let them choose their birthday luncheon, but otherwise it is so much easier for all if you cook what you want to cook. It's nice if it's a treat from Daddy who cooks something different for each child occasionally for breakfast, but as a full-time parent you must decide what you are making or it becomes an impossible life for you – a slave short-order chef. Of course if you are providing yoghurt for pudding and your child wants a different flavour from the one you have provided for him I would certainly look for the flavour he wanted – you must treat the child as you would an adult with respect to food. One time I would differ with children from my treatment of adults is, for instance, if you are staying at a hotel with more than one child. If the children are under six I would simply order the same meal for each child and not even let them see the menu because it creates chaos.

A mother of two (seven and four years old) contacted me in despair. Her children's dislikes were legion. They would even say 'I don't like that' before they had tasted it. The younger one was taking his cue from his elder sister. She didn't know how to stop the situation, whether to with-hold puddings if they didn't eat their main course or just to say 'Sorry, this is it for today - take it or leave it'.

I reassured her that children could go for a long time with very little food so she shouldn't worry if they didn't eat their main course. I said she should certainly not withhold pudding as it was part of the meal and could be eaten even if the main course was not eaten. I told her to serve the first course and if they ate it then fine, if they didn't I would take it away and then serve the pudding. The most important thing was not to discuss it. If they didn't want to try something then she shouldn't even put it on their plate – it would be a waste of good food. The problem would be solved much quicker by not giving them anything they didn't want to eat. I reminded her that adults don't have to try things if they don't want to – children should be allowed the same sort of respect.

## More of what he fancies

There are children who enjoy eating very much and I would always let them have more. If a child particularly likes the beans and yet doesn't want to finish the mince he can be offered a few more beans. There's an old saying 'His eyes are bigger than his tummy' (a child may have enjoyed something so much that he wants more and yet when he gets it he isn't able to finish it). But I wouldn't worry that if a child ate more of his main course he wouldn't have room for his pudding. If he is enjoying his main course and wanted some more then I would allow him to have some and would give him a very small helping of pudding to start with.

## Mealtimes should be peaceful

Often when babies fuss about their food it is because there is too much else going on in the room and they are distracted. I always try and feed babies and young toddlers on their own so we can have a very peaceful time and they can concentrate on the job in hand (see Chapter Two). I aim for a civilised, friendly, enjoyable atmosphere at mealtimes, sitting down at the table with the family. In very many homes today this traditional pattern of behaviour has almost disappeared. You see adults reading over their meal, older children helping themselves to things from the fridge to eat on the hoof and younger children with a plate on their knees while sitting on the sofa watching television. A TV supper or having television on at mealtimes is neither civilized nor peaceful. How can one enjoy food to the full in a family situation if heads keep turning to the television set?

Often, when a child has been called to the table from his play, he would want to bring a new or a favourite toy to the table. I had a very strict rule, I never allowed toys on the table. I would put it on the shelf under the high-chair and say 'You can play with it later' or sometimes I have put it on a chair somewhere else in the room and said 'We don't want it on the table, I'll put it here and then you can see it whilst you are eating'.

You don't want toys all over the place. I have seen children who will have bunny or dolly wedged into their chair and will offer dolly a spoonful once they have had theirs. This is very sweet but it can take such a long time and I do think mealtimes should be enjoyable for all, brothers, sisters and adults as well as the child. He can feed dolly afterwards.

## Don't let him play with food

Sometimes children feeding themselves play with the food, stirring it round at a great rate so it is spilt. In that case I would remove it and then the child would shout and wave his arms about and want his food back. Quite soon, a few minutes later, I would put it back and help him eat it and politely ask him not to play with it again. I think if it happens at the end of the meal and the child is playing with his jelly and obviously not very hungry I would just remove it.

## No snacks between meals

I think the main reason why children don't eat their meals is often that they are so full of drinks and biscuits and crisps and sweets and chocolate that they have no appetite to eat their food. If they are slightly hungry they do enjoy their food so much and it causes less tension all round. An infuriated parent who makes a nice lunch that the child doesn't eat can only blame herself if she has let the child fill up with snacks or fruit drinks or milk. As I never give a child anything at all to eat between meals – unless we are on the beach and they have an ice-cream – my children never ask for food. However, sometimes visiting children do and then, of course, you have to give them a biscuit if that is what they are used to, but it does ruin a child's appetite. I don't suppose it matters if the child wants to eat lots of snacks during the day, providing they are nutritious, but it is a tremendous nuisance for the mother and I don't think it is necessary. After a long night a child will have a very hungry tummy and if he then has a big breakfast it should keep him going until lunch time.

$A$ very familiar problem is the one of the two-year-old child who used to eat everything and now wants nothing except potato crisps and biscuits between meals. One mother told me of her two-year-old who had recently started just picking at his food and refusing to finish it, but when he got down from the table he demanded biscuits and bread sticks.

Sitting on the side lines it is easy to say that he wouldn't have known about biscuits and bread sticks if he hadn't at some stage been given them, but as this had started I suggested that the mother gave her son a small helping of food at each meal which he might eat or might not and she shouldn't make him eat it if he didn't want to. Once he had eaten as much as he needed then she should take his plate away and give him his pudding. After the meal he should be given nothing. When he got down and asked for a biscuit, she shouldn't give him anything at all, she should just calmly say 'Well I'm sorry, you must wait until tea time' and if he gets very upset he will just have to get upset. I told her she needn't feel sorry for him, he won't be hungry. Very soon he will eat more when he is sitting in his chair and get used to eating three good meals a day again. I told her there is no need to pander to him at meal times either and cook special meals that she knows he likes so he won't be hungry. Whatever she is going to eat he can eat too and if he doesn't want to it doesn't matter.

## No filling up with drinks

Left to their own devices children would drink and drink. If there's a drink available they will pick it up and drink it right to the bottom and it fills up their tummies and then they have no room for their meal. I would never give children more than a little mug of fruit juice to drink between meals unless it was a hot day and they asked for it, when I would give them a drink of water. I give them a drink of fruit juice first thing in the morning and from the age of two in the middle of the morning as well and then a drink at the end of each meal otherwise they do get full of liquid and don't eat so much food.

I never even put a jug of water on the table until after the meal unless someone specifically asked for it, but that was rare. I probably said 'Finish your pudding and then I'll get you a drink'. Otherwise they would have a very long drink if they were that thirsty and then might not finish their pudding which was something I would rather did not happen. At the end of the meal I would give each child a drink. If they have always had their drink at the end then they accept it. It is essential that children enjoy good food and they won't be able to if they have too much liquid before they start eating.

# CHAPTER SEVEN

# My Tried and Tested Routines

B Y THE TIME YOU READ THIS BOOK YOU WILL HAVE already formed a routine with your baby. If it is your first child this may be flexible to some extent to fit in with other demands on your time, but if there is an older child you will have all the more need of a routine because having a small baby is in itself such a time-consuming experience. If you have a particular routine which allows for all these demands it really does help. I followed this routine all my working life – it applies for bottle- and breast-fed babies.

## New Born Baby To Four Months

### A. M.

**2.00** (or whenever he wakes) Breast- or bottle-feed and nappy change. Then back into his crib.
(If he does not wake I would not wake him.)
**6.00** Breast- or bottle-feed and nappy change. Then back to sleep in his crib.

**9.30** Bath, then clean nappy and clothes.
(If awake. If not, I would leave him to sleep until 10 a.m., but no longer.)
**10.00** Breast- or bottle-feed, then back into his pram.
(He would probably be awake and looking around perfectly happily before going to sleep.)
**11.00** Put him in his pram.
(Indoors or outdoors, depending on the weather. If you need to go shopping or to the park then you could do it now.)

## P. M.

**1.00** Nappy change and change of scene.
(If I hear him shouting I would turn him around in his pram or I would bring him in and put him on the floor of the playpen under a mobile to give him a change of scene. If he was really fed up I would feed him a little bit earlier.)
**2.00** Breast- or bottle-feed and nappy change.
(Unless you have fed him earlier, see above.)
**2.30** Put him in his pram.
(See 11 a.m.)
**4.00 – 4.30** Fruit juice (once he is six weeks old).
(I wouldn't wake him up for his fruit juice, but babies usually do seem to be awake by now. After that I put him on his back in the playpen or on a rug on the floor so he could look around. If he is restless and grizzles it means he is hungry or tired, so I would move on to feed and bed earlier.)
**5.30 – 6.00** Top and tail.
**6.00** Breast- or bottle-feed. Then into his crib.
(If you can, make this a cosy time, wrapped up in a shawl, all by yourselves, with a dim light for company.)
**10.00** or **11.00** Breast- or bottle-feed and nappy change, then back into his crib.
(Either wake him for this feed or leave him to sleep until he wakes up hungry.)

# Five Months To Eight Months

For the next four months the routine remains the same with only one change each month which is to slowly introduce a baby to solids and wean him from the breast or bottle.

## Five months old

**10.00 a.m.** Replace the breast or bottle with a cup.
(I allow weaning from the breast to take four months – I think it is unkind to do it any quicker.)

## Six months old

**2.00 p.m.** Solid feed and replace the breast or bottle with a cup.
(I now introduce solids and replace the bottle or breast with a cup for the second feed.)

**Two weeks later**
**10.00 a.m.** Solid feed followed by milk from a cup.
(I now introduce a baby cereal for breakfast.)

**A week later**
**6.00 p.m.** Solid feed followed by bottle- or breast-feed.
(I now introduce a baby cereal for tea.)

## Seven months old

**1.00 – 2.00 p.m.** Solid feed followed by milk from a cup.
(I now introduce two courses – a main course and a pudding for lunch followed by milk from a cup.)
**5.30 – 6.00 p.m.** Solid feed followed by milk from a cup.
(I now replace the bottle or breast with a cup for the third feed.)

### Eight months old

**6.00 a.m**. Replace the breast or bottle with a cup.
(I now replace the bottle or breast with a cup for the fourth feed. Do not wake your baby for this feed. Unless he wakes up he does not need anything until breakfast which can then be given at 8 a.m. as in the following routine.)

# Nine Months To One Year

## A . M .

**7.00** Fruit juice and nappy change then back to bed with a few toys.
(This may be earlier or later depending on when your baby wakes up.)
**8.00 – 8.30** Breakfast, then pot, then play.
(Once a baby is nine months I put him on the pot so he gets used to it. Then he plays – either in his playpen or out of it – depending on whether he can walk.)
**10.00** Put him in his pram.
(Indoors or outdoors depending on the weather. If you need to go shopping or to the  park then you could do it now.)

## P . M .

**12.00 – 1.00**  Lunch, then nappy change or pot, then play.
(From eleven months I would put the baby on the pot after lunch as well as after breakfast and tea.)
**2.00** Go to the park.
(We would go to the park for two hours unless the weather was bad. When we came home I would make tea and the children would play in the nursery. If  you had to go shopping this would also be a good time.)

**4.00 – 5.00** Tea, then pot.
(Once the baby was ten months old I put him on the pot after tea as well as after breakfast.)
**5.00** Play.
**6.00** Bathtime.
**6.30** Drink of milk, then bed.
(Until a baby is nine months old I always feed him last thing at night as I don't think it is fair that he should have his last meal at 6 p.m. Once he is over nine months I would give him a drink of milk now, but only if he asked for it.)

# One Year To Five Years

For the next four years the routine remains more or less the same. Gradually he will be sitting on the loo rather than having to have his nappy changed, his meals will get larger and he will need less sleep. The main change in routine comes with the introduction of school.

## One year old

**6.30 p.m.** Bed and story.
(At this age I stop giving the baby a drink of milk at bedtime because he has had a mug of milk at tea-time. If he is thirsty then I would give him a drink.)

## Two years old

**10 a.m.** Go to the park.
(I no longer put him out in the pram, instead I take him to the park for an hour – or you could go to the shops now if necessary.)
**11 a.m.** Juice and rest.
(Once we had returned from the park he would go to bed for an hour before lunch.)
**12 p.m.** Lunch, then rest.

(After lunch I would put him in his room with a book for roughly an hour, sometimes he fell asleep and sometimes he didn't. He would be quite happy just to be on his bed. Then he would play in the nursery before we went out to the park.)

## Three years old

The routine continues as for the two-year-old unless your child is starting nursery school when it will need some juggling around.

## Four years old

**9.00 a.m.** Play.

(Either in the garden or in the nursery.)

**11 a.m.** Juice and reading lesson.

(With a blackboard we would do letters and numbers. I taught all my children to read when they were four.)

**11.15 a.m.** Park.

(We would take a ball and meet other children.)

**1 p.m.** Lunch then rest.

(No nap was necessary but some children get tired quicker than others. I would put him to bed with a book and sometimes he would just sleep.)

# CHAPTER EIGHT

# Some
# Possible
# Problems

S OME PROBLEMS ARE, OF COURSE, NOT OF A PARENT'S making. Your child may be allergic to certain foods or he may become ill. Either of these situations can make feeding him difficult. The important thing is to give your child good, nourishing, simple food. There are many things that he would be much better without; if someone gave a nine-month-old baby a chip, he would suck it and swallow it and he wouldn't drop dead, but it is much more sensible to give a baby of this age food that is easy for his stomach to cope with.

## Children and allergies

Where I was trained we had a little eighteen- month-old girl who couldn't eat potato – it made her sick. Her mother asked one day 'Does she like potato? I could never eat potato because it made me sick.' Isn't it extraordinary, that something like that could be hereditary? Very often things do run in families, intolerance of a specific food and so on. If in your family there is a particular food allergy you will watch out for it, but even if there is not, new foods should always be introduced slowly so you can then know if the child has any reaction to them.

Some children do have allergies which must, of course, be respected and taken note of, but they are not the norm. An allergy may be indicated if a child's lips, eyes or face swell or he has a rash on his body or his face, or both, or an unusual amount of wind.

Allergies are much rarer than some people acknowledge, however. There are some children who are allergic to dairy products. You would know by now if your baby was allergic to the dairy products you ate when you were breast-feeding him but there are some babies who might not have minded that but when they start on cow's milk, they cry and cry – all day and all night. If this happens then you must go to your doctor who will probably suggest that you give your baby soya milk. Only one of my ten children was allergic to anything – egg. One day I noticed her face was rather rough, it was obviously not as it should be and I wondered if it could be the egg. The next time she had egg the same thing happened, so I discussed it with the doctor and we decided to withdraw eggs from her diet. Her complexion cleared up. I waited a year and then tried egg again and she was all right. One would have thought that if she was allergic then she would always be allergic, but she wasn't. Some people are allergic to peanuts; peanut butter can make them feel depressed and, more seriously, peanuts can make them choke or irritate their lungs. I wouldn't give a child nuts before he was five. Others are allergic to pulses or chocolate, but these are exceptions and the people who have these allergies learn how to avoid them.

## Coeliac disease
The likelihood of your child having Coeliac disease is

very remote, but if after starting solids your baby's faeces are especially offensive in smell and if there is a great deal of wind making the tummy distend and if your baby doesn't seem to be putting on weight I would certainly ask the doctor. Coeliac disease is an illness in which the lining of the small intestine is sensitive to gluten, causing faulty food absorbtion. This means that the baby must eat a diet which is free of gluten, a protein found in grains such as wheat, oats, barley and rye.

## Foods to avoid

Fashions come and go as to which foods should be avoided. I was taught never to give a child a banana, even a mashed one, before he was two as it was thought this fruit was indigestible but now I would certainly give a child a very ripe banana, beating it up with a fork so it was nice and mushy. When I was young people were frightfully keen on giving children lots of sugar to give them energy, now we think otherwise, probably because too much sugar certainly does contribute to tooth decay. Raw eggs are now considered a health hazard and honey, they say, considered health giving for thousands of years has been found to contain botulism toxins. It is very difficult to come to terms with all these new food scares.

### Oranges, chocolate, ice cream

Oranges or undiluted orange juice should not be given to a baby under the age of one because they may cause itching, swollen eyes or diarrhoea. Before a child was two I never gave him any chocolate. This is easy to do with the first child and impossible with subsequent children, although it is worth trying. I wouldn't give a child an ice cream or ice lolly before they were at least two-and-a-half and then only when we were at the sea-side.

**Indigestible foods**

If children eat baked beans, raisins or sweet corn you will notice that these foods pass whole through the child. So I would never serve them to a child under the age of three unless I put them through a sieve or mashed them because if they come out as they go in they obviously haven't nourished the child in any way. Before the age of five children were not given salty or spicy food, although once they were eating with the family they would eat small amounts of salt in the cooking. We first gave children ham and bacon when they were five. Pastry and cheese were reckoned to be indigestible, and were also only to be introduced to a child's diet at this age. I would also never give shellfish to a child under five in case it caused a severe allergic reaction and stomach upset.

## The sick child

Sometimes if there has been a difficulty or a tantrum or something it may mean that the child doesn't eat very much, but I don't take any notice. Or often when they are tired they don't eat very much either. I just give them a little more for their next meal and don't remark on it. An ill child will also eat very little, usually only for a very few days. He may be cooking up chicken pox and if he doesn't eat for a few days it doesn't matter as long as he drinks a lot - he will soon catch up once he is well. If you are worried I would always ask the doctor as there are glucose drinks you can give him if he is very weak and doesn't want to eat.

*I* once heard from a mother who was worried because her 11-month-old daughter brought up her food every time she had a cold. She would eat but would be sick either straight after her meal or a little later and yet she was still gaining weight. For over a week she had hardly eaten any food and was gagging at every mouthful because she had such a blocked nose. Her mother wondered if she should stop trying to feed her until her cold was better.

I said that if her daughter didn't want to eat then she shouldn't make her but otherwise she should continue to provide the food. Very often children with colds are sick after eating because there is mucus in the tummy. When the child is sick, up comes the food and the mucus she is swallowing. I told the mother that it was not real vomit although there probably is a little food in it. I said that if her daughter continued to gain weight there was no need to worry, but that it might be worth offering some more food once she had been sick.

## Do I go on weighing my child?

Once a child is one he should have trebled his birth-weight. After that I don't weigh him any more unless there are other things that worried me, the fact that the child is lethargic, eats very little, is unhappy, cries a lot - anything that would disturb me that isn't the norm. I think I would then weigh the child twice a week so that I could monitor what is going on. But this is an extreme case – if the child is happy, running about and sleeping all night it is quite unnecessary to weigh him, even if he eats less than you would like him to. There are fat people and thin people and children take after one or the other parent. There are plump babies who turn into thin adults and the other way round. If they have had a satisfactory year then there is no need to weigh them unless you are worried for some other reason.

# A note from Nanny

By now your child's whole eating pattern is fairly established. Some children have big appetites and some smaller and I would follow the child's lead. If he wants more of something I always give it to him although sometimes it is difficult to know if he wants more as most children when they have finished their plateful pick up the plate and hold it out to you. Until they can tell you clearly you don't really know if they want more or not, so I wouldn't give them a second helping of the first course unless it was plain that they wanted more, otherwise there would be no room for their pudding. Of course, there may not be any more left 'All gone'. Quite often they mean more food; they are still hungry but will be just as happy with the pudding as with more main course.

I hope this book has helped you to enjoy meal times with your baby. I am sure you will find it very satisfying when your child enjoys the food you have made for him. On the other hand, do not be offended when he refuses it. Babies really do know best.

Good luck!

# What to Feed
# Your Baby

T HE LIST OF LUNCHTIME MEALS THAT FOLLOWS, ONE for every day over three months, is just a guideline, ideas which you may find useful. This is the way I started mixed feeding with my children. You don't have to prepare the food yourself, you can use jars or tins. Make sure the age on the label is suitable for your child. Or you can make a large helping of each dish and divide it into little pots and freeze it. I used to steam or poach most of the food I was cooking or use a pressure cooker.

I first introduce fish when the child is almost nine months. He eats between one and three eggs a week – the yolk only at first and then I slowly begin giving him the white. The cheese I give him is a very mild cheddar cheese.

Babies often like their puddings more than their main course so I sometimes give them alternate mouthfuls of main course and pudding if I can feel him resisting the main course.

# Lunch Menus – Six to Nine Months Old

Before feeding, always check that the food is not too hot for the baby. At the end of each meal your child will be having a drink of milk, whether from breast, bottle or cup (see Chapter Three).

## *Six months*

### Week 1
| | |
|---|---|
| Monday | Apple purée (see page 49) |
| Tuesday | Apple purée |
| Wednesday | Apple purée |
| Thursday | Apple purée |
| Friday | Apple purée |
| Saturday | Apple purée |
| Sunday | Apple purée |

**Note**: I give the same food at lunchtime throughout Week 1 to accustom the baby to the new experience of mixed feeding.

### Week 2
| | |
|---|---|
| Monday | Carrot purée (cooked and sieved) |
| Tuesday | Carrot purée |
| Wednesday | Apple purée |
| Thursday | Carrot purée |
| Friday | Apple purée |
| Saturday | Carrot purée |
| Sunday | Apple purée |

### Week 3
| | |
|---|---|
| Monday | Spinach purée (cooked and sieved) |
| Tuesday | Spinach purée |
| Wednesday | Apple purée |
| Thursday | Carrot purée |
| Friday | Spinach purée |
| Saturday | Apple purée |
| Sunday | Carrot purée |

## Week 4

| | |
|---|---|
| Monday | Apple purée |
| Tuesday | Carrot and spinach purée and apricot purée (cooked and sieved) |
| Wednesday | Parsnip and potato purée (cooked and sieved) and prune purée (cooked and sieved) |
| Thursday | Carrot and potato purée and mashed banana (beaten until liquid) |
| Friday | Swede and potato purée and apple purée |
| Saturday | Potato and cauliflower purée (cooked and sieved) and apricot purée |
| Sunday | Carrot and parsnip purée and prune purée |

# 7 months

## Week 1

| | |
|---|---|
| Monday | Potato purée mixed with lightly boiled egg yolk and apple purée |
| Tuesday | Apricot puree with semolina pudding |
| Wednesday | Spinach purée and egg custard (sugar not necessary, just use egg and milk) |
| Thursday | Potato purée with finely grated hard cheese and prune purée |
| Friday | Parsnip with potato purée and mashed banana |
| Saturday | Carrot and potato purée and apricot purée |
| Sunday | Spinach and potato purée and apple purée |

## Week 2

| | |
|---|---|
| Monday | Carrot and spinach purée and apple purée |
| Tuesday | Parsnip and potato purée and egg custard |
| Wednesday | Swede and potato purée and mashed banana |
| Thursday | Carrot purée with finely grated hard cheese and prune purée |
| Friday | Potato and parsnip purée and apricot purée |
| Saturday | Potato and carrot purée and apple purée |
| Sunday | Potato and swede purée and semolina pudding |

## Week 3

| | |
|---|---|
| Monday | Carrot and spinach purée and apple purée |
| Tuesday | Parsnip and potato purée and prune purée |
| Wednesday | Carrots and potato purée and apricot purée |
| Thursday | Potato and cauliflower purée and apple purée |

| Friday | Potato with lightly boiled egg yolk and semolina pudding |
| Saturday | Spinach and potato purée and apple purée |
| Sunday | Potato purée with grated cheese and apricot purée |

## Week 4

| Monday | Potato purée with lightly boiled egg yolk and milk jelly (fruit jelly made with milk and water - add the milk when the liquid is cold) |
| Tuesday | Potato with chicken purée (cook and then mince or liquidize) and prune purée with custard |
| Wednesday | Potato purée with grated cheese and junket (made with rennet) or custard |
| Thursday | Carrot and parsnip purée with yeast extract and apple purée |
| Friday | Potato purée with lightly boiled egg yolk and apricot purée |
| Saturday | Potato and sprout purée with grated cheese and mashed banana |
| Sunday | Carrot and potato and chicken purée and semolina pudding with apricot purée |

# 8 months

## Week 1

| Monday | Potato and Brussels sprout purée with lightly boiled egg yolk and apple purée |
| Tuesday | Chicken with carrot and potato purée and apricot purée |
| Wednesday | Potatoes and parsnip purée with grated cheese and milk jelly |
| Thursday | Potatoes and carrot purée with yeast extract and prune purée with semolina pudding |
| Friday | Spinach with cauliflower purée with lightly boiled egg yolk and apple purée |
| Saturday | Potato and Brussels sprout and chicken purée and apricot purée |
| Sunday | Swede and carrot purée with yeast extract and mashed banana |

## Week 2

| | |
|---|---|
| Monday | Potato purée and lightly boiled egg (see if he has any reaction to the whole egg) and semolina pudding with apricot purée |
| Tuesday | Potato purée with grated cheese and apple purée |
| Wednesday | Spinach and potato and chicken purée and junket |
| Thursday | Potato and Brussels sprout purée with lightly boiled egg and mashed banana |
| Friday | Carrot and potato and parsnip purée and apple purée |
| Saturday | Parsnip and potato purée with grated cheese and apricot purée with custard |
| Sunday | Swede and potato purée with lightly boiled egg and milk jelly |

## Week 3

| | |
|---|---|
| Monday | Potato and chicken and spinach purée and mashed banana |
| Tuesday | Parsnip and carrot purée with yeast extract and apricot purée with custard |
| Wednesday | Potato and carrot purée with lightly boiled egg and junket |
| Thursday | Swede and cauliflower purée with grated cheese and milk jelly |
| Friday | Parsnip and potato and chicken purée and apple purée |
| Saturday | Swede and potato purée with yeast extract and mashed banana |
| Sunday | Potato and Brussels sprout purée with lightly boiled egg and prune purée with custard |

## Week 4

| | |
|---|---|
| Monday | Potato and spinach purée with grated cheese and junket or custard |
| Tuesday | Carrot and potato purée with yeast extract and apple purée |
| Wednesday | Parsnip and Brussels sprout purée with lightly boiled egg and semolina pudding with apricot purée |
| Thursday | Spinach and potato purée with mashed or liquidized steamed white fish and prune purée with custard |

| Friday | Swede and potato and chicken purée and mashed banana |
| Saturday | Potato and carrot purée with grated cheese and apple purée |
| Sunday | Potato and spinach purée with yeast extract and milk jelly |

# Balanced Meals – Nine Months to Two Years Old

Until the child is eighteen months old, all his food is puréed. After that it is mashed together with a fork rather than a sieve or blender. Only once he is two do I begin to serve his food cut up into small pieces.

Until a child was two we used to give him a lot of offal (especially liver, brains and tripe) as it was considered to be more nutritious than the flesh of an animal. If you are worried about giving your child these foods you can always check with your doctor first. We also gave children herring roes, another food which is good for them. When you give fish to children you must be very sure you have removed all the bones first. We always ate stoneground wholemeal bread; when serving this to children I would remove the crust from the bread until the child is two. At the end of breakfast and tea, I give a child a small mug of milk and after lunch a drink of water (see Chapter Five).

First, a drink of fruit juice on waking

**Breakfast, 8.00 - 8.30 a.m.**
**Day 1** Scrambled egg. Toast with butter and yeast extract
**Day 2** Porridge. Toast with grilled tomatoes
**Day 3** Baby cereal. Grilled herring (or fish fingers) with wholemeal bread and butter

**Day 4**  Prunes. Toast with butter and honey
**Day 5**  Boiled egg with soldiers (strips of toast to dip in the
egg). Toast with butter and jam
**Day 6**  Porridge. Rusks with butter and honey
**Day 7**  Grilled herring (or fish fingers). Wholemeal bread and
butter with syrup

or **Quick Breakfast**

Cereal or porridge. Occasionally stewed fruit or yoghurt. A bit
of wholemeal bread toast or crust to chew with a little butter
and honey, yeast extract or syrup.


## Lunch, 12.00 p.m. - 1.00 p.m.

**Day 1**  Poultry or grated hard cheese with baked potato
(remove the skin and mash with a little butter and a
little milk) and green vegetable. Baked or fresh grated
apple with yoghurt

  or **Quick Lunch**

  Baked potato with grated hard cheese and courgettes.
Baked apple with yoghurt

**Day 2**  Steamed or stewed calves' or lambs' liver (or minced
lamb), and cabbage and potato. Banana custard

  or **Quick Lunch**

  Minced lamb with mashed potatoes and carrots.
Banana with yoghurt

**Day 3**  Baked or boiled egg, shell removed, with potato and
baked tomato or green vegetable. Semolina pudding
or rice pudding and raw grated apple or pear

  or **Quick Lunch**

  Pasta with tomato sauce and grated cheese. Raw
grated apple and milk jelly

**Day 4**  Steamed white fish with parsley and courgettes or
carrots or boiled beetroot and potato. Steamed
sponge pudding with syrup or bread and butter
pudding and raw apple.

  or **Quick Lunch**

  Fish fingers and mashed potatoes with parsley and a
vegetable. Junket (made with rennet) or crème
caramel and raw grated apple or pear

**Day 5**  Minced meat (lamb or beef or chicken) with potato or
rice and spinach. Fresh fruit salad with yoghurt or
fruit yoghurt.

or **Quick Lunch**

Unspiced sausages and potatoes or rice and spinach. Fruit yoghurt

**Day 6** Lentil and vegetable soup with wholemeal bread and cream cheese. Sponge pudding or plain sponge cake with fruit purée

or **Quick Lunch**

Baked beans on wholemeal bread. Apple crumble

**Day 7** Fish pie with parsley sauce with carrots and greens. Stewed fruit with yoghurt or egg custard

or **Quick Lunch**

Macaroni cheese with a vegetable. Milk jelly (packet jelly made with milk instead of water)

# Tea 4.00 p.m. - 5.00 p.m.

**Day 1** Rye crispbread with yeast extract. Fresh fruit jelly and sponge cake

**Day 2** Grated cheese and carrot with brown bread and butter. Mashed banana

**Day 3** Oatcakes with butter and tuna fish. Yoghurt with prunes and a sponge finger

**Day 4** Fingers of wholemeal toast, some spread with honey and some with yeast extract. Stewed fruit and cake

**Day 5** Fresh tomatoes with wholemeal bread spread with butter and yeast extract. Scone with honey and a fresh apple

**Day 6** Fingers of wholemeal toast spread with mashed sardines and pieces of tomato. Stewed fruit and a piece of sponge cake

**Day 7** Oatcakes with butter and mashed dates. Plain cake and raw apple

or **Quick Tea**

Selection of the following : Rusks; crusts of wholemeal bread; postage-stamp sized sandwiches with yeast extract, dripping, syrup, honey, jam, egg, cress or tomato; Madeira cake, sponge cake, plain biscuits or shortbread; fresh or stewed fruit or a bowl of baby cereal

# Index

# INDEX